The Lockback Knife
From Design to Completion

**Peter Fronteddu
and Stefan Steigerwald**

Schiffer Publishing Ltd

4880 Lower Valley Road, Atglen, Pennsylvania 19310

Other Schiffer Books on Related Subjects:

Basic Knife Making: From Raw Steel to a Finished Stub Tang Knife • 978-0-7643-3508-2 • $29.99

Translated from the German by Christine Elliston.

Originally published as *Back-Lock-Messer: Von der Konstruktion zum fertigen Klappmesser* by Wieland Verlag.

Copyright © 2010 by Schiffer Publishing Ltd.

Library of Congress Control Number: 2009943047

Designed by Stephanie Daugherty

Type set in Dutch809 BT/Zurich BT

ISBN:978-0-7643-3509-9
Printed in China

Schiffer Books are available at special discounts for bulk purchases for sales promotions or premiums. Special editions, including personalized covers, corporate imprints, and excerpts can be created in large quantities for special needs. For more information contact the publisher:

Schiffer Publishing Ltd.
4880 Lower Valley Road
Atglen, PA 19310
Phone: (610) 593-1777
Fax: (610) 593-2002
E-mail: Info@schifferbooks.com

For the largest selection of fine reference books on this and related subjects, please visit our web site at

www.schifferbooks.com

We are always looking for people to write books on new and related subjects. If you have an idea for a book please contact us at the above address.

This book may be purchased from the publisher.
Include $5.00 for shipping.
Please try your bookstore first.
You may write for a free catalog.

In Europe, Schiffer books are distributed by
Bushwood Books
6 Marksbury Ave.
Kew Gardens
Surrey TW9 4JF England
Phone: 44 (0) 20 8392 8585
Fax: 44 (0) 20 8392 9876
E-mail: info@bushwoodbooks.co.uk
Website: www.bushwoodbooks.co.uk

Contents

A Few Introductory Sentences

Creating all kinds of folding knives is one of my greatest interests. So many individual parts work together and result in a functioning system. The fit, combination, and design of each knife always present a new challenge. Many problems arose while making the knives in this book, but were resolved as easily as possible. With each issue we faced Peter Fronteddu asked me how and why I handled the problem the way I did—much has become natural for me. My approach to the problems, which we discuss in this book, should not be considered absolute, but make the lockback knife lock system comprehensible. This frees the knifemaker from predetermined designs and encourages experimentation. Is there anything better?

Stefan Steigerwald

First and foremost, I would like to thank Stefan Steigerwald. It was pure luck that I was able to work with a bladesmith with vast technical knowledge who can realize his design concepts in so many ways. As a non-bladesmith and observer, I hope the text and pictures allow the reader to see how the fundamentals of designing and constructing a lockback knife became clear to me in the course of my collaboration with Stefan Steigerwald.

Many things are not as simple as they seem when looking at a finished knife. In contrast to industrial manufacturing, when constructing individual handmade pieces, improvisation; instinct; and; above all, patience are necessary. For me those are the intrinsic values of a completed knife; for me, it is what makes a handmade knife appealing. The more I learn the more I can appreciate it.

Therefore, I hope that this glimpse behind the scenes of knife making also interests those who do not intend to pursue the hobby. And I encourage those who are inspired to tackle your first project!

Peter Fronteddu

1. Initial Thoughts

1.1 General Considerations

There is not a single proven method for designing and constructing a lockback knife. In this book we describe the production of a particular knife, but also discuss alternative design features and production methods. We use concrete examples throughout the process—from the first sketch to a completed knife.

We will also discuss the basic technical qualities of a lockback knife. These are the constants that are necessary for proper function. The specific way these technical aspects are executed is left up to you, the knifemaker. Our book is not necessarily a manual for "the one" method, rather, we want to provide you with a technical foundation that you can use to implement your own ideas.

This approach includes introducing various production methods and knife designs, a gallery of which you will find at the end of this guide. Not everyone can or wants to use extensive and expensive machinery. Therefore, in various sections we will identify other solutions and techniques using simple means.

We must include a brief note on work safety. Because we documented the individual steps photographically, necessary and practical safety measures were partly spared. Anyone making a knife should become familiar with the necessary measures that guarantee a safe work environment beforehand, especially when power tools are being used.

1.2 The Knife

Before making any initial sketches, we should define the basic components of the knife. Our example should be a pocket-friendly knife. Therefore, we define the length of the blade at approximately 90 mm. It is also important that no edges protrude outwards on a completed knife.

The construction should be screwed together and not riveted. This has various advantages. First, mistakes made during production can be easily corrected since you can access and re-work the individual parts. Second, a knife that is screwed together is easier to clean. Finally, you can later replace individual parts (washers, springs, etc).

For the locking device we have chosen two basic variations. The first style features a device that extends far toward the back of the knife and locks at the end of the handle. For the other variation, the lockback is released toward the middle of the handle. We will show both options, as well as different versions for the locking spring.

Knife Anatomy

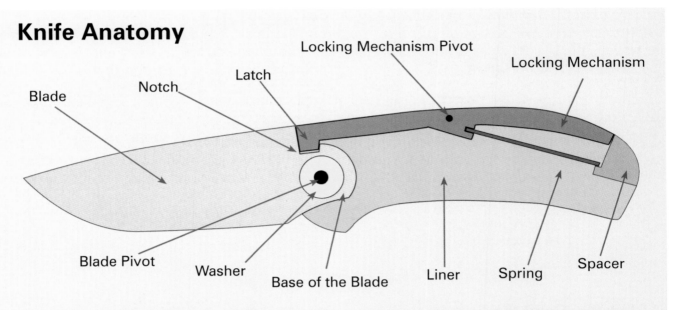

In the classic version of a lockback locking mechanism, the locking mechanism extends over the entire length of the handle. There are also shorter versions.

1.3 Material Selection

Typically the first thing to consider when making a knife is the correct type of steel to use for the blade. For our pocketknife we are planning to use a steel that is easy to handle and is available in the required dimensions. In addition, the material should not be too costly to finish, it should be easy to grind to a fine cutting edge, have strong edge retention (i.e. hardness and carbide distribution), and be rust-resistant. Furthermore, the material should be affordable.

Selecting steel is always a compromise. A suitable material is one that meets each requirement as much as possible. Therefore, our choice is RWL-34, the powder-metallurgical variant of ATS-34. For the decorative version of our knife, however, we have decided on an industrially produced, powder-metallurgical Damascus steel with a fine visual appearance.

Naturally, there are many options when selecting steel. Unfortunately, a detailed discussion of steel is not in the scope of this guide.

We do, however, have some advice for making the proper decision. The question of steel is primarily a question of taste. Make your decision based on personal preferences, how you will use the knife, your decorative interests, options for treatment, and price. There is no correct or incorrect decision.

The variety of steels available to the knifemaker has increased considerably in recent years. There is now a range of non-alloy and low alloy carbon steels (1095, CK60, CK 75, 1.2842, and others). They form fine cutting edges, have a high hardenability, and are sufficiently stable at the cutting edge. Carbon steels are easy to handle, heat treat, and grind—and they are rather inexpensive. Their main disadvantage is that they are not rust-resistant (in fact, there is really no such thing as a rustproof, hardenable steel).

For the knifemaker who places value on rust-resistant knives, high alloy steels containing chromium, such as ATS-34, 440C, 154-CM, AUS-8, and 12C27 are available. Normally the advantage of rust-resistance comes at the expense of having a cutting edge that is not as fine as a carbon steel blade. High alloy steels at the same hardness as a carbon steel tend to be less stable, which, however, does not play a huge role with the dimensions of our pocketknife blade.

High alloy, rust-resistant steels that are produced in a powder-metallurgical process go one step further. During this manufacturing process many small, evenly distributed carbides form. These carbides create elasticity and edge retention that exceeds that of carbon steels or conventional chromium steels. In comparison, the high alloy steels that are not produced with powder metallurgy form larger and unevenly distributed carbides. These could break out in the cutting edge and lead to microscopic nicking. This phenomenon creates a fine saw tooth, which is well suited for a pulling cut if that is what you are looking for.

Another material to consider is Damascus steel. Due to the revival of bladesmithing in recent years, a large selection of hand forged Damascus steels are now available. The Swedish company Damasteel, for example, uses powder metallurgy to produce a rust-resistant Damascus steels.

Today the use of Damascus steel is more a question of aesthetics. Even with high quality industrial steels, made by blending various types of steels, a performance edge can hardly be achieved. And with hand forged Damascus steels, which are made specifically to improve performance, a possible improvement in quality is incommensurate to price and effort. That is not fundamentally an argument against using Damascus steel—individuality cannot be measured, even with a price.

What is generally missing from discussions regarding steel are the questions of heat treatment and cutting edge geometry. Like material selection, both characteristics have the same effect on cutting performance. Only with appropriate heat treatment does the steel obtain its desired characteristics—hardness, flexibility, fineness of the cutting edge, and rust-resistance. A heat treatment that is not optimal eliminates the potential benefits of the steel. Therefore, only use a steel for which you understand the heat treatment process—regardless of whether you harden the steel yourself or give the steel to a heat treatment workshop.

Blade geometry has a decisive influence on the cutting ability and robustness of the blade. The edge angle determines the force needed for cutting i.e. the smaller the edge angle, the sharper the blade and the less pressure you need to cut with the knife. On the other hand, the cutting edge must correspond to the steel and its usage. With high alloy steels there is the danger of carbides breaking out with a cutting edge that is too fine.

Conclusion: when selecting a steel, only considering the type of steel is cutting the issue short. Instead, in choosing your steel, you must reach a compromise between steel type, heat treatment, and blade geometry.

We left the heat treatment of all blades discussed in this guide to a heat treatment workshop that has experience with knife blades and the types of steel we plan to use. The results from this particular shop are advantageous because the blades are hardened in a vacuum furnace, which significantly reduces the amount of scale (an oxide layer) that we will need to grind off. Before sending the blade to this shop for hardening we can nearly complete the finishing and satin-finishing process. We find it sufficient to leave 0.2 mm to 0.4 mm on the cutting edge before hardening.

We will complete the frame of our knife with 2A1V pure titanium. Titanium is light, very stable, completely rustproof, and changes color. The spring-tempered titanium 6A14V is more difficult to work with and does not offer any advantages for our purpose. The liners for the knife are 2.0 mm thick. This gives the knife its desired stability and provides enough material for the thread that we have to cut into the liners.

For the bolsters we will use powder metallurgical RWL-34 steel that, together with the blade, is hardened at 59-60 on the Rockwell scale (HRC). In a hardened state the steel is less susceptible to scratches. For the decorative version we will make the bolsters from Damascus steel. There are many optional materials for the bolsters (i.e. mokume, brass, nickel silver, bronze, etc.). Choose one that fits the quality and appearance of the blade and the handle scales.

Like the bolsters, the choice of material for the handle scales is a matter of taste. For the different versions of our knife we have chosen stabilized wood, mother of pearl, bone, mammoth ivory, and meteoric iron. As a basic principle the handle material should correspond to the quality of the knife. You should also pay attention to the material's longevity so that the hard work you put into developing accurate fittings is not lost. Therefore, with wood we suggest using stabilized materials or a very hard wood (i.e. desert ironwood, grenadilla, boxwood, or ebony).

Take note, many materials that are often used for handmade knifes have hidden health risks and require extra precautions when handled. Dust and other particulate matter from many tropical woods and composite materials are toxic or at least allergenic.

In particular, stabilized woods contain acrylic resins and mother of pearl contains arsenic. Also, carbon fibers are respirable. The use of suitable respirators and exhaust systems is strongly recommended. Retailers who offer knifemaking supplies should be able to help with the selection of suitable materials and answer questions on proper handling.

For our locking mechanism we will use RWL-34 or 1.4034, each brought to blade hardness. For the inserted springs we will use spring steel 1.4310 (rustproof spring steel strip) with a 40-45 HRC hardness. Alternatively, spring steels made of carbon steel are also available. These are not rustproof and therefore have a higher hardenability, which causes more stress in the material. Knifemaking supply stores should carry suitable round or flat stock. In the back of this guide you will see another version of the lockback knife, for which we constructed the locking mechanism and spring from a single component, the rust-resistant 1.4034 steel, hardened and tempered at approximately 45 HRC.

For screwing together the parts of a knife, high-grade steel is recommended, preferably of V2A or V4A quality. We will use TX6 torx cylinder head screws. The heads are partially striped for a slim visual appearance. For our knives the outer diameter of the heads is sized 3.8 mm to 3.0 mm. Part of the screws should be gold-plated—you have to spoil yourself some times.

The blade pivots are made from titanium, primarily for visual reasons. Alternatively, you can make pivots out of brass or steel. Brass has good anti-friction properties, is easily obtainable, and easy to work with. We should point out that your pivot material must be approximately five to ten HRC degrees softer than the blade. Because little pressure is placed on the blade pivot in the rotational direction, the question regarding material for the blade pivots is rather non-critical. Smooth blade action, however, is essential.

2. Design, Sketch, and a Functional Template

2.1 Design Fundamentals

A pocketknife should be made for daily use. It should be small enough to fit in your pocket but large enough to take care of everyday tasks. A blade length of around 90 mm is a good compromise. Depending on the design, a finished knife should have an effective cutting length of approximately 70 mm. We will later grind the entire width to achieve an optimal cutting angle at the cutting edge.

2.2 Concrete Design Elements

The basis of our design is the classic lockback variation. The locking mechanism for this knife is operated at the end of the handle. We will add bolsters to the handle to protect the handle scales underneath, visually extend the blade, and give the knife a high-quality look. Alternatively, scales can be added over the entire length of the handle.

To be able to adjust the blade play in the completed knife, the blade pivot screw should be visible and accessible from the outside. In the design gallery at the end of this guide we show a knife that has a pivot concealed by the bolsters and handle scales. While this certainly has a cleaner appearance, you must unscrew the bolsters and handle scales to adjust the blade play.

When sketching your knife, make sure that the knife's edge is flush when closed and that no edges, for example the blade ramp, protrude from the handle. Furthermore, your knife should have a consistent line from the spine of the blade over the scales.

This basic template will allow you to make multiple variations of the lockback locking mechanism.

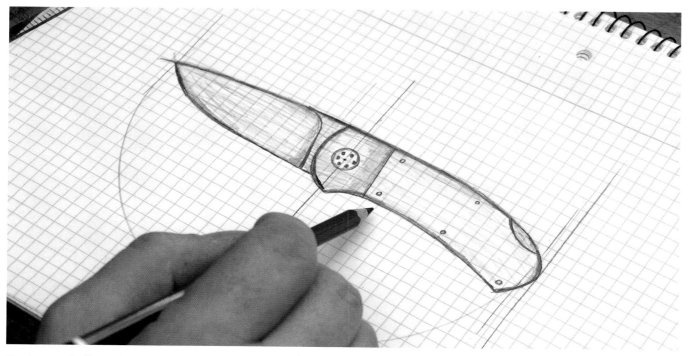

Begin your knife making with a sketch. Draw guidelines to determine the maximum length of the blade.

2.3 Creating a Functional Template

Functionality of a Lockback Locking Mechanism

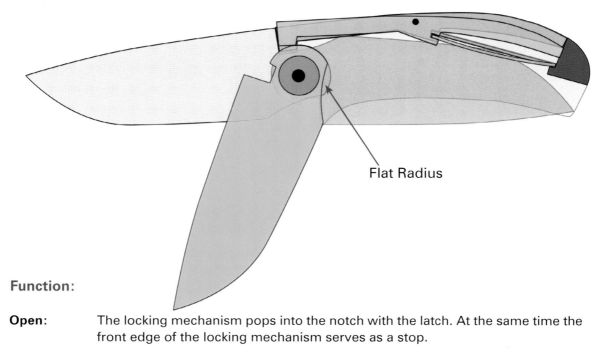

Flat Radius

Function:

Open: The locking mechanism pops into the notch with the latch. At the same time the front edge of the locking mechanism serves as a stop.

Open/Close: The lock is released. The latch runs on the radius of the blade base under spring pressure.

Closed: The blade base hits the inside of the locking mechanism. With spring pressure the latch lies on the edge of the flat radius and holds the blade in the handle.

With the construction of a lockback locking mechanism the knifemaker has various options. The locking mechanism can extend through the entire body and be operated at the end of the handle. For this, an appropriate notch is incorporated in the liners. Alternatively, a shorter locking mechanism can be used that is operated from the middle of the handle. The exact position is a matter of taste.

For a long locking mechanism there are numerous options for the design of the spring:

1. The spring (round or flat stock) is placed into the locking mechanism on one end and rests on a spacer or appropriate support pin on the other.

2. The spring and locking mechanism form one piece. To ensure it has the functionality of a spring, this type of locking mechanism must be made of the relevant material with the proper heat treatment. The other end of the spring rests on the spacer or a support pin.

3. The spring (round or flat stock) is placed into the spacer and pushed onto the locking mechanism from the bottom.

4. The spacer and spring form one unit. The spring pushes on the locking mechanism. The spacer must be made of a material that can function as a spring.

5. An additional option would be to use a coil spring that is placed into the spacer and works on the locking mechanism from the bottom.

Version 1: Locking mechanism, spring, and spacer are separate parts. The spring is placed in the locking mechanism and rests freely on the lip of the spacer.

Version 2: The locking mechanism and spring form one piece. The spring rests freely on the lip of the spacer.

Version 3: The spring is placed in the spacer and runs freely along the locking mechanism.

Version 4: The spring is placed in the locking mechanism and runs freely on a stop (dowel pin, roll pin, etc.), which serves as a spacer and secures the liners.

Version 5: The spring and spacer form one piece. Under pressure, the spring rests on the locking mechanism with a slight curve.

Version 6: Instead of a flat spring or leaf spring, a coil spring is used. It rests on the spacer and presses on the locking mechanism.

Version 7: Short locking mechanism. As an alternative to the long locking mechanism, you can use a short one. The control lever is placed near the middle of the handle.

All of these methods are suggested, but for our knife we will use a slightly curved flat spring that presses on the locking mechanism and is held in the spacer with a notch, as in Version 1 above.

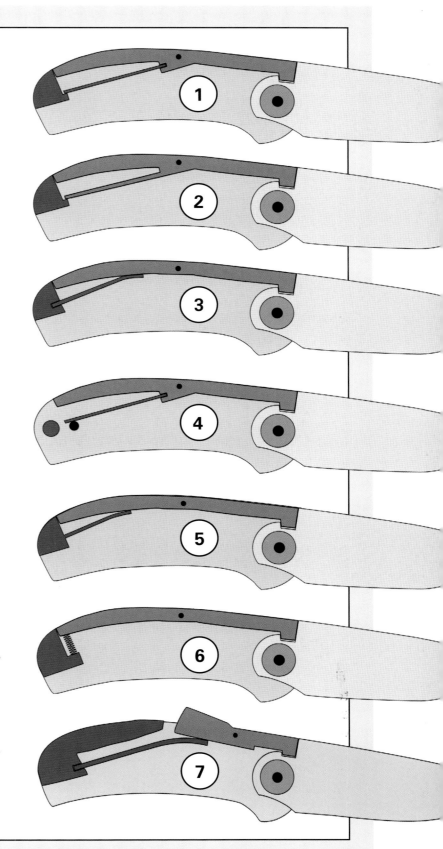

In principle it is best to make the spring a single component and place it in the spacer of the locking mechanism. You are not as limited in the materials you can select for this part and the construction method is more fault-tolerant (with incorrect measurements of the spring you only have to replace this one part). Also, the spring is easily replaced should it happen to break or lose its springiness.

In all of these versions the construction of the actual locking mechanism—the area of the latch and blade ramp—is identical.

Open knife: The latch reaches into the notch of the blade and locks the blade. The front edge of the notch must rest as far forward as possible but not protrude over the outline of the liner. The back edge of the notch (made at an 8° angle) is the actual contact surface during locking. At the height of the pivot center it should be positioned closer to the back edge.

Closed knife: When closing the knife the lower surface of the latch lies spring-loaded on an edge on the base of the blade and presses the blade into the frame. This edge must rest in front of the blade pivot (toward the tip of the blade). The farther forward the edge is worked in, the stronger the blade is held in the frame (due to the leverage). The depth of penetration for the latch can also be relatively freely chosen. On one hand, the lock should secure. On the other hand, the lever must be moved this way (here the position of the notch, the gear ratio, plays a roll once again). For us, the depth of penetration is approximately 2.0 mm. To have more play with the adjustment, we will make the notch in the blade somewhat deeper so that some space remains between the latch and the bottom of the notch. For our knife the latch should sit approximately 2.0 mm deep in the notch. To provide sufficient stability, the width of the latch should be approximately 5.0 mm.

There are varying opinions regarding the correct angle of the surfaces. It is important to note that when the latch is in use, it moves in a circular motion. If one works exclusively with right angels, the latch could potentially get stuck on the ramp, it will not penetrate far enough and get caught when opened. Therefore, the back edge must be at an angle. In our case we are using an angle of between 8° and 9°.

The front side of the notch is 90°. In some knifemaking manuals a slight taper of 4° to 5° is suggested for the back of the notch. However, because completing such a small angle is quite complex without proper machinery, we have abstained from doing this for our knife. Restrictions in capacity were unnoticed.

First, sketch your design. You do not need exact measurements. Later we will test the knife's operation with a functional template. As a rule, the length of the blade in a folding knife cannot be longer than the handle (except for the so-called "extension knife"). Draw in the pivot and stop pin.

Leave space in the blade spine for the locking mechanism and in the spacer for the inclusion of the spring. Therefore you must choose the width of the blade appropriately. When closed the blade should not reach too far toward the spine.

With this sketch you should establish the basic structure of your knife. Once you have the design, transfer the sketch to cardboard. During this step consider the knife's functionality along with the blade's outline, locking mechanism, the stop of the closed blade, the position and measurement of the spacer, the shape of the blade ramp, and the position of the blade pivot. You should also include a rough sketch of the recess in the handle, where the locking mechanism will later operate.

For the functional template, use an adequately thick and stable cardboard. We will use it extensively throughout the knife making process. In addition to serving as an operational test for your knife, your template should also give you a good feel for the ergonomics of your knife.

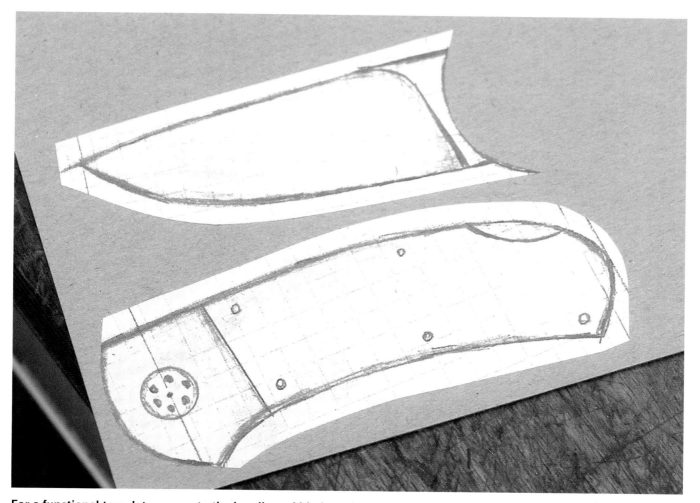

For a functional template, separate the handle and blade and adhere to cardboard.

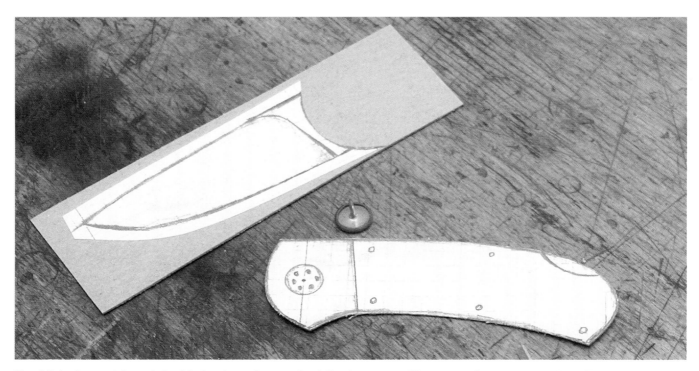

Establish the position of the blade pivot. As a makeshift pivot, we will use a tack on our template. The pivot point is located slightly below the midline.

Glue the sketch to the cardboard and cut out the templates for the handle and blade. When you cut out the blade, leave some material at the end to later test the position of the pivot and finish the outline of the blade ramp. Position the blade pivot just below the midline of the handle to have enough space for the locking mechanism in the back of the handle.

Place the blade pivot far enough toward the back so that the blade and washer have a sufficient contact surface. The blade can be shortened if you set the pivot closer to the rear of the knife. You will need to find a suitable compromise. Here is some helpful advice. The distance from the blade pivot to the upper edge of the handle should correspond approximately with the distance from the pivot to the front edge.

Place a tack through the handle and blade template in the determined location and pivot the blade into the handle.

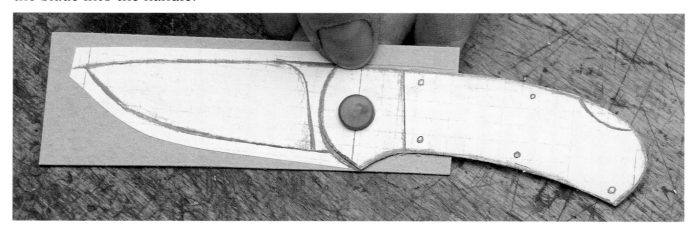

Using a tack, assemble the blade and the handle piece.

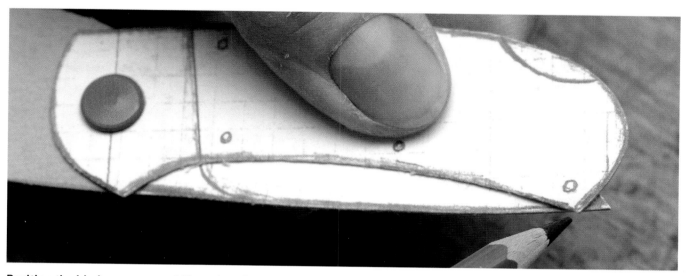

Position the blade as you would in a closed knife. If the tip of the blade extends beyond the length of the handle, shorten it accordingly.

On the backside draw the outline of the cutting edge onto the handle when the knife is folded. Some space remains up to the back of the handle. We will use this space later for our locking mechanism, spring, and the spacer, on which the spring is affixed.

Position the blade as you would in a closed knife. If the tip of the blade extends beyond the length of the handle, shorten it accordingly by drawing the outline for the cutting edge onto the inside of the liner. That is the maximum space that you will have for the locking mechanism, the springs, and the spacer. If you determine that the space is too tight, you can adjust the blade at this point.

Then cut out the blade ramp along the handle. The blade should not overlap when the knife is closed.

Take apart your template again and begin planning for the lock. The latch should have a height of 5 mm and engage 2 mm deep into the notch in the blade. To do this draw a circle around the pivot, the upper point of which is 5 mm from the spine of the blade. Later the latch will run on this circle when you open and close the blade.

Left: So that the blade ramp (when the knife is closed) does not extend over the handle, we trace the outline of the handle on the blade. **Right:** Cut out the blade along the line. This establishes the area we have available for the blade ramp.

A Multifunctional Part

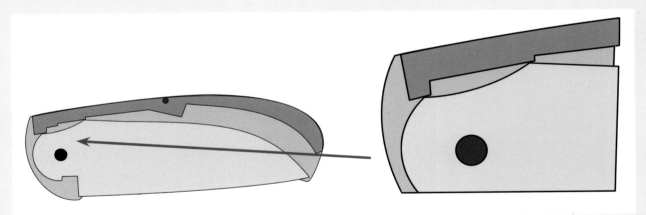

In addition to locking the open blade, the locking mechanism assumes two other functions:

1. **Holding the blade closed**: The latch presses on the back edge of the radius, pulling it into the handle.

2. **Locking the blade when the knife closes**: The blade rests on an edge of the lock behind the latch. Leave some material at the base of the blade and the inside of the locking mechanism to make fine adjustments to these parts.

Alternatively, or to make up for mistakes during production, an additional stop pin can be placed into the liners.

Trace guidelines outlining the notch where the latch will rest. Later you will see how the latch pulls the blade into the handle when the knife closes. This can only work if the latch is applying pressure at the blade pivot. Therefore, the latch must engage at the blade pivot when open.

Draw a line through the center of the blade pivot, perpendicular to the midline of your knife. The latch should lock 2 mm deep in the blade, so we trace another guideline perpendicular to the first, 2 mm below the top of the radius.

Sketch the notch. For this we draw a front and back boundary line. The front edge of the notch lies as far forward as possible, but not beyond the outline of the handle. From the top of the pivot, start by sketching the back edge of the notch, using the required 8° angle.

Sketch the radius where the latch will run. The blade pivot is the center point and the top of the circle should start 3 mm below the spine of the blade.

The latch should engage the handle at an angle of 8° to 9°.

With the traced radius and our guidelines, the outline of the notch is complete.

Cut out the notch and neatly cut around the radius on your blade template, leaving some cardboard in the lower right hand corner. This is where the closed blade rests on the locking mechanism and will need to be adjusted.

Assemble the blade and handle with the tack and open the blade to see how the blade locks into the handle. Using the notch you just cut out, trace the latch and the front section of the locking mechanism on the inside of the handle.

Now fold the blade and finish sketching the locking mechanism. It reaches backwards over the recess in the handle. Mark the fulcrum of the locking mechanism, which is close to the center of the handle. The position of this point determines how much or little force is necessary to release the lock. The start of the spring is just behind the fulcrum.

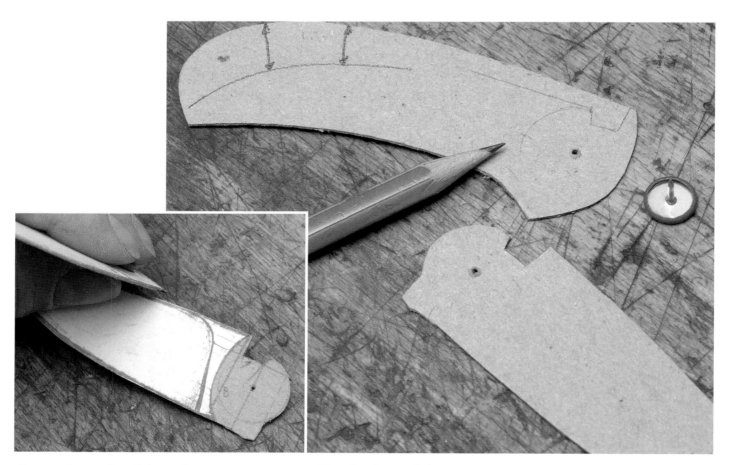

Cut out the notch and the radius.   **Transfer the notch from the blade to the handle.**

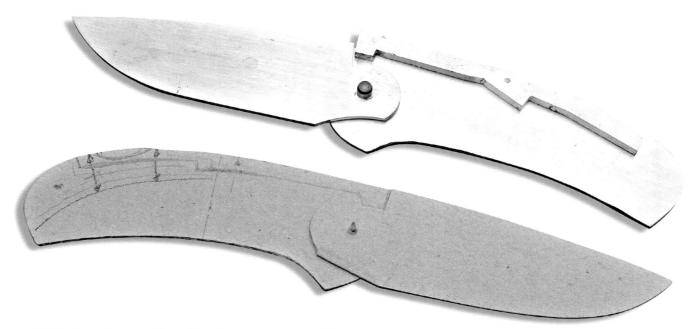

In addition to making a cardboard template, we suggest making another template from aluminum or brass. In the above template we made the locking mechanism a separate component and connected it to the handle using a dowel pin as a pivot.

Next we draw the spring that presses on the locking mechanism from below and the spacer at the end of the handle.

You can also finish the blade lock on the template. When the knife is closed the blade ramp should rest on the locking mechanism at an angle. The cutting area of the blade should not hit against the locking mechanism. Piece by piece we complete the blade ramp and locking mechanism.

Using the template, adjust the outline if necessary. It is important to work as precisely as possible and make any adjustments at this stage, before you start constructing the actual knife. In particular, we must create clean junctions between the handle and the blade when the knife is open. Precise measurements will also guarantee that the blade lock functions properly, locking the latch in the notch when the blade is open and securing the blade against the locking mechanism when closed. In the open and closed positions the locking mechanism should neatly lock with the back of the handle. If the latch does not engage safely when the knife is open, adjust the bottom side of the knife correspondingly. Leave sufficient space for the mechanics.

Correct Angles for the Notch

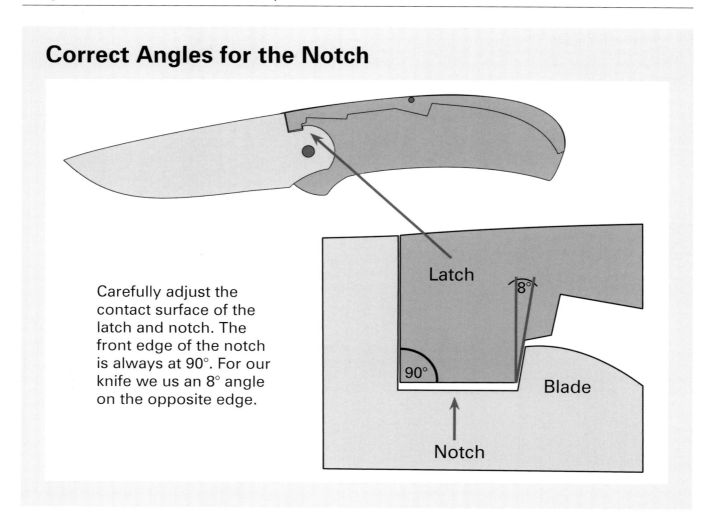

Carefully adjust the contact surface of the latch and notch. The front edge of the notch is always at 90°. For our knife we us an 8° angle on the opposite edge.

Latch

8°

90°

Blade

Notch

Advice: All of these design features affect each other reciprocally. Therefore, if you make any changes during construction, you must check all functions again!

There are a few critical points where you should leave some excess material: the point where the latch locks into the blade (open) and the ramp where the blade rests (closed). This is a question of method. Because we want to make a functional brass template in addition to our cardboard template, we have decided to work with templates that are as precise as possible.

Naturally, you can also complete your knife's design using a computer. If you have access to the necessary hardware and software, such as a CAD program, you can make accurate and functioning mock-ups of your design. When making a lockback knife it is very helpful to have a functional template to test and adjust. Cardboard is easier to work with and cheaper than steel. Finally, with a functioning template you can get a good feel for the ergonomics of your knife.

We will make a brass template based on the cardboard template we created. The brass offers advantages; first, adjustments are made more precisely. Second, a brass template is more durable. If you plan to use the same template to make several knives, the initial additional expense for the brass is recommended.

3. Producing the Liners

Working With Dowels

When it comes to accurately positioning the spring, locking mechanism, and spacer, dowel pins are used to fix these parts to the knife. Generally, screws are not always enough because they do not always hold the components in place. A dowel pin, however fixes the components in the correct positions.

To accurately mount the dowels, clamp and drill the components that need to be fixed in the knife. Clamping the components together at the same time allows you to keep the drilling angle consistent. Drill under size because we will later ream to the exact measurement of the dowel pin. For 2.0 mm dowels, drill with a 1.8 mm and then ream to 2.0 mm. This guarantees that the dowel stays fast in the drill hole.

The materials for our knife cut to size.

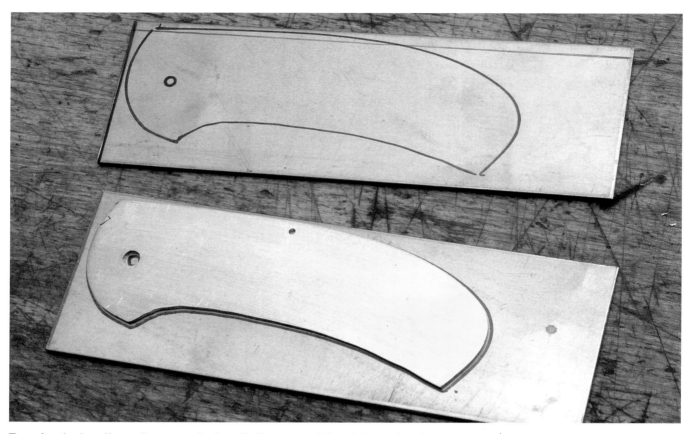

Transfer the handle outline onto the handle liner material and draw the pivot.

Drill the pivot hole with a 3.8 mm bit.

Cut the handle liner material to size. Then transfer the outline of your template onto the titanium plate and mark the position of the pivot.

We will later produce a pivot with a 4.0 mm diameter. For this we pre-drill into both liners with a 3.8 mm bit and then ream the drill holes to 4.0 mm.

Grease the drill holes with cutting oil before reaming them.

Ream the 3.8 mm hole to 4.0 mm exactly.

Fix the two liners together by placing a dowel pin through both pivot holes and applying instant adhesive. Then trace the outline of the liner onto the flat stock. Because we handled both liners at the same time, the pivot holes will later be placed exactly across from each other and the pivot will not tilt.

Now that the liners are affixed you can cut them out of the metal. First, use a hacksaw to make a rough cut. Then use a drill press to drill the material out along the marked edge of the liner. You can use a fretsaw to cut out the remaining material. Once you have a rough cut of the liners, file the edges until they are smooth, finishing the outline with a belt grinder. Finally, finish the edges with a grinding surface loaded with 240 grit abrasive paper.

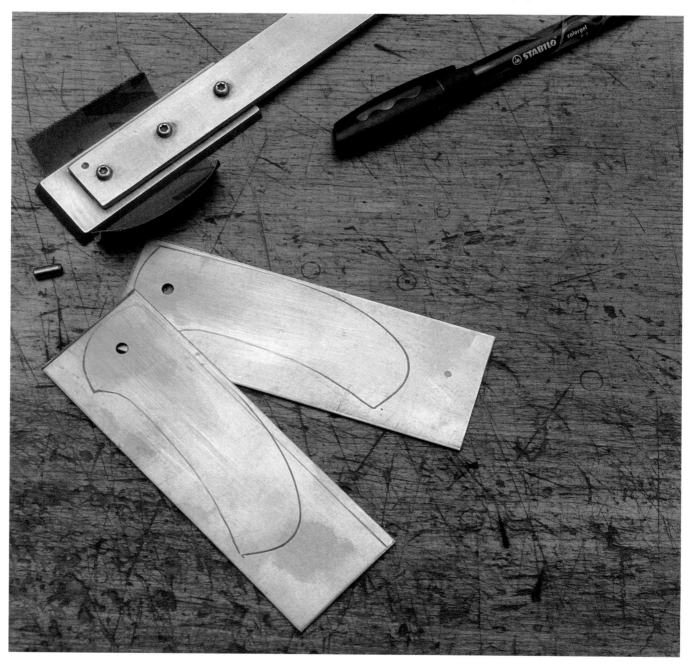

Sketch the outline for the handle.

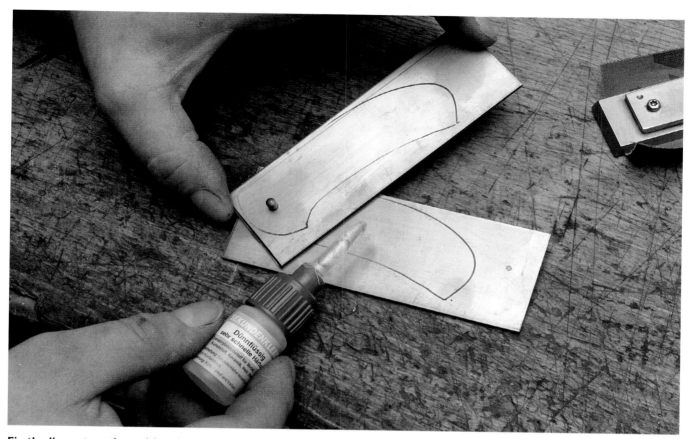

Fix the liners together with a dowel pin and instant adhesive. Then cut out the joined pieces.

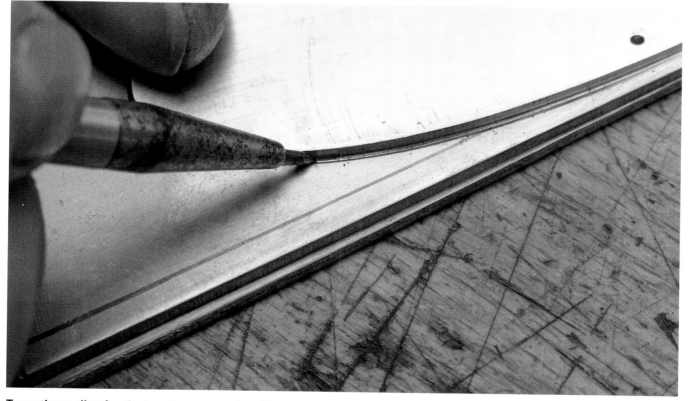

Trace the outline for the handle once again with a brass needle.

Clamp the liners together to cut the liners with a hacksaw.

The hacksaw gives you a rough cut of the liners. The precision work follows.

Saw away as much excess material as possible so that you have less to file or grind away.

The round inner contours of the liner are difficult to reach with a hacksaw. Therefore, drill a series of holes, close together along the outline.

Cut through the remaining material with a fretsaw.

Continue finishing the contours of the piece with a file.

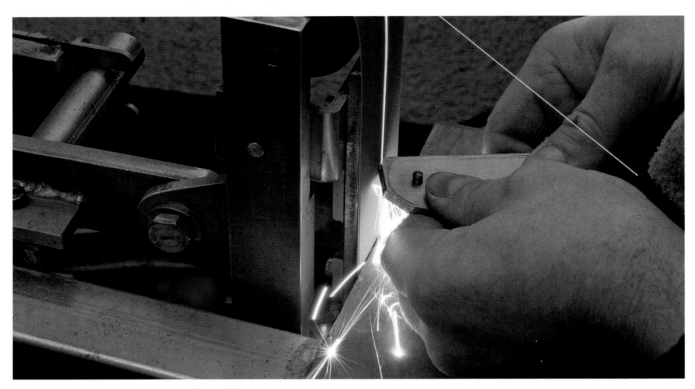

Alternatively, use a belt grinder (80 grit).

No matter how you manage the preliminary work, neatly finish the liners by hand (up to 240 grit).

Using your template, trace the finger tab that will operate the locking mechanism and file it out. Again, the finishing work is done with 240 grit abrasive paper until the desired outline is reached and no file marks are visible.

Transfer the position and shape of the finger tab from the template to the liners.

Work out the finger tab with a half round file.

Clamp abrasive paper (240 grit) onto round stock with the same radius as the tab and file the surface.

Finally, grind the liners once more to achieve a clean surface.

4. Making the Blade

Place the blade template onto the flat stock and trace the outlines. If you are making multiple knives, draw two different blade outlines.

Mark the hole for the pivot on the stock as well. Then pre-drill the holes for the pivot with a 3.8 mm bit and ream to 4.0 mm. Assemble the template once again and mark the blade outline. With the help of a dowel pin, place the blade blank onto a liner and check your outline. If the height fits with the back of the handle, is the length of the blade correct?

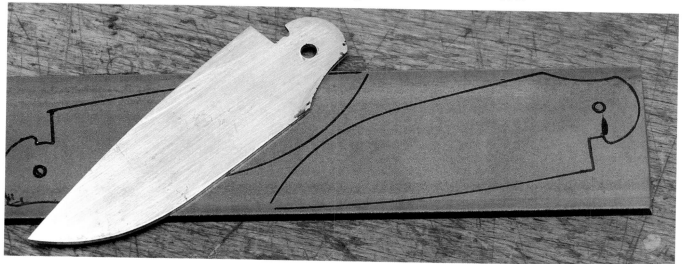

Transfer the blade outline and the hole for the pivot to the blade steel.

Like the pivot hole on the liners, pre-drill the hole with a 3.8 mm bit.

After greasing with cutting oil, ream the drill hole to 4.0 mm.

With a dowel, assemble the blade template and mark the blade outline.

Trace the blade outline onto the blade steel.

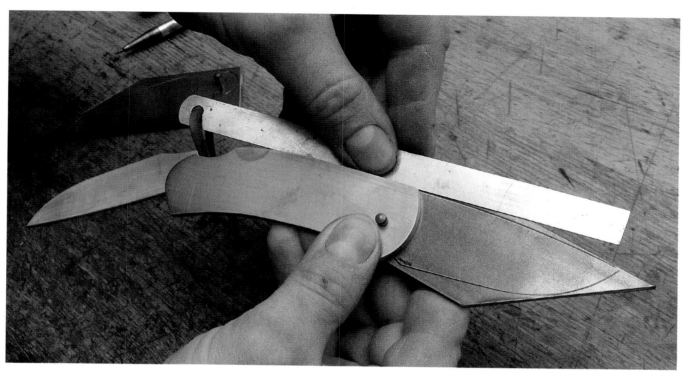

Join the blade with the handle liner and check the outline of the blade before proceeding.

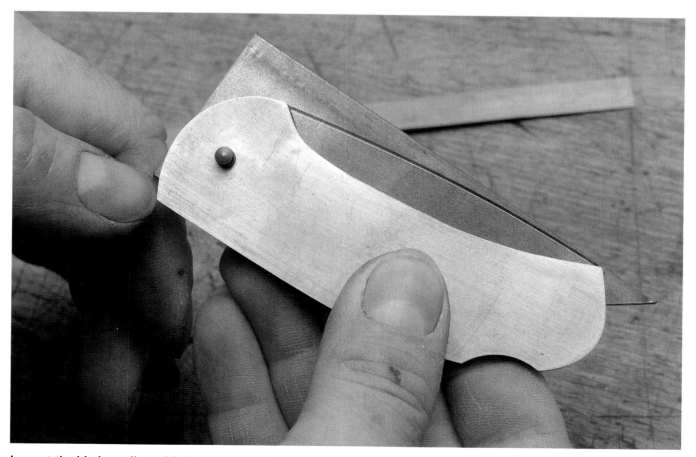

Inspect the blade outline with the knife folded as well. The handle must cover the notch, the spine of the blade should be consistent, and the tip of the blade should not extend beyond the back of the handle.

Rough cut the blade steel with a hacksaw or cut-off wheel, establishing the shape of the blade as you did with the handle liners.

Like the handle liners, use a hacksaw for a rough cut on the blade.

You can also drill a series of holes along the outline.

Cut through the remaining material with a fretsaw.

A rough outline develops.

Remove excess material with a file and continue to work out the outline.

Another option for rough cutting the outline of your blade is using an angle grinder equipped with a thin cutting disc.

Leaving some excess material on the blade lock and the recess for the locking mechanism at this point will help you later when you go to fine-tune the functionality of your knife.

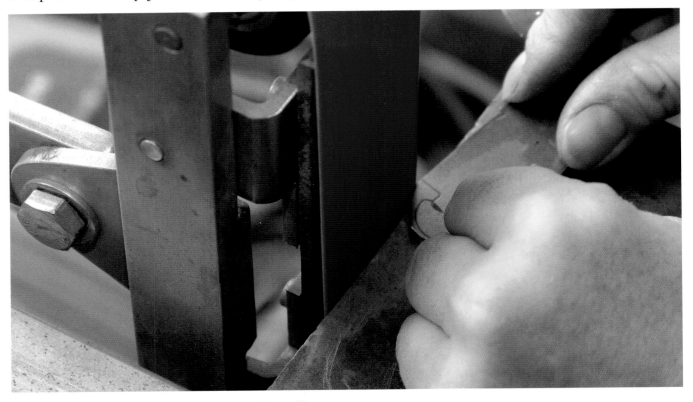

Use a belt grinder if available, as it is faster than a file.

This is what your rough blade blank should look like. You can clearly see the leftover material on the notch and base of the blade.

The first step to creating a functioning locking mechanism is to develop the blade. We will finish the latch and the remainder of the locking mechanism, as well as the interior surfaces in later stages. The final adjustments take place after hardening the locking mechanism, a process that may cause distortions. Adjustments made prior to hardening may no longer be accurate after the process. Making sure the locking mechanism fits onto the blade is less costly than the reverse method.

Like our template, we first create the radius on which the latch will run. The latch should have a height of 5 mm and sit 2 mm into the blade. Leave a little bit of space and establish the radius at 6 mm. The center of the radius is the center of the blade pivot.

To achieve a neat radius on the tail of the blade, clamp it onto the rotary table of a milling machine. Use a locating pin for a clean alignment.

Clamp the blade onto the rotary table.

Mill the radius on the rotary table with an end mill.

You can also file the radius. To do this we prepared a round tool to keep the blade pivot aligned with the center of the radius. The round tool has the same diameter as the radius. Several markings on the tool help you accurately file and grind along the radius. Finish the radius with 240 grit abrasive paper.

We created a locating pin for filing the radius at the base of the blade.

The round tool helps us maintain the shape of the radius during filing. We added several marks on the tool to see when the shape of the radius is complete.

Good results can be achieved with simple means.

Because the latch of the locking mechanism runs along the radius, the blade pivot must be placed exactly in the center of the radius. Also, make sure the section of the radius that contacts the locking mechanism is smooth. You should not leave any rough file marks on the piece. We recommend finishing with a 600 grit paper or higher.

Now we will make the notch. First, mark the notch's position using our template. Place the blade on the handle and draw the front edge of the handle on the blade. The notch cannot be positioned in front of this mark.

The width of the notch is determined by the desired width of the latch, 5 mm in our case. Make sure the front edge of the notch is in front of the center point of the pivot so that the latch pulls the blade into the handle when the knife is closed and holds it in place. Mark a guideline across the height of the blade indicating the front edge of the notch. Mark a similar guideline extending from the back edge of the bottom of the notch to the pivot. This line should align with the center of the pivot.

Next, determine the depth of the notch. The latch should dip down 2 mm, but leave some extra space at the bottom of the notch to better adjust the latch in later steps. The depth should be between 2.5 mm and 3.0 mm, measured from the top of the radius down.

Remember that the angle of the rear ramp in the notch should be 8°. When you mill, however, mill sharper than this because we will remove more material in subsequent steps. Use a 4.0 mm end mill bit to produce a latch with a width of 5 mm.

To clamp the blade exactly level, mark a contour line on the blade that runs perpendicular to your previous guidelines. Clamp the blade along this line in the vise on the milling machine. First, mill along the front edge of the notch to approximately 2.5 mm to 3.0 mm below the top of the radius. Then mill the rear edge of the notch to the bottom of the notch at approximately 8°.

So the latch runs smoothly on the surface, touch up this area using a file and abrasive paper (up to 600 grit). To maintain the angle on the rear edge, mark the angle on the blade and clamp it in the vise.

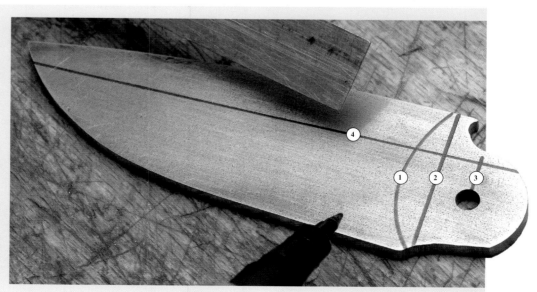

Mark the dimensions for the notch:

1. Front edge of the handle

2. Front edge of the notch (must be behind the front edge of the handle)

3. Extension of the pivot center (approximate end of the notch)

4. Contour line (determines the depth of the notch and serves as a reference point for clamping the blade in the vise)

Mill the front edge of the notch at a 90° angle.

Mill the rear notch at an 8° angle.

If you prefer to work without a mill, you can file out the notch. Here we are filing out the front edge. The vise holds the blade in place and maintains the right angle.

Mark a guideline and clamp the blade at an angle to file the rear edge.

Use a file to work out the rear edge. The vice helps once again.

Regardless of whether you use a mill or file, all surfaces should be neatly finished by hand (up to 600 grit).

The blade is now finished up to the inner curve, where the stop will rest when the blade is closed.

5. The Locking Mechanism

For the locking mechanism we will use RWL-34 and 1.4034 as a variant. The steel type 1.4034 is also well suited for the version in which the lock and spring are made from a single piece. If springs are inserted, any common blade material can be used for the locking mechanism.

The locking mechanism should be at least as thick as the blade plus both washers. To avoid lengthy grinding work, the dimensions of the raw material should be as close as possible to this measurement.

Place the blade loosely into your liners and roughly sketch the outlines of the blade onto the locking mechanism in the notch area. As before, leave a little excess material when working on this section so you can make adjustments later.

Here we temporarily assemble the blade with a dowel pin. Adjust the raw material for the locking mechanism accordingly, inside the handle outline.

First, mark the notch and the base of the blade on the locking mechanism.

The marked material. This will later become the latch of the locking mechanism.

Extend the traced line for the latch to the edge of the material.

Mark a clamping guideline perpendicular to the line you just marked.

The front edge of the latch should dip down into the notch at a 90° angle. Mark a corresponding guideline and work out the edge by filing or grinding. Then mill or file the bottom of the latch. Finish the front 90° edge with a 600 grit abrasive paper.

Clamp the locking mechanism in using your long guideline.

Mill the front edge and the bottom of the latch. You could also file this edge.

Finish the milled surfaces by hand (up to 600 grit).

Adjust the rear edge of the latch at an angle using the notch in the blade as a guide. Clamp the blade accordingly in the milling machine or work out the edge with a file. If working with a file, it is best to clamp the blade in the vise with the help of a guideline marked at an appropriate angle.

Work step by step, regularly checking the fit of the latch in the notch. The latch should not dip down completely but sit 2 mm in the notch. Finally, finish all mating surfaces of the latch with abrasive paper (600 grit).

Clamp the locking mechanism along the guideline and set the mill at an 8° angle. Regularly checking the fit with the notch, you will reach the correct dimensions for the latch.

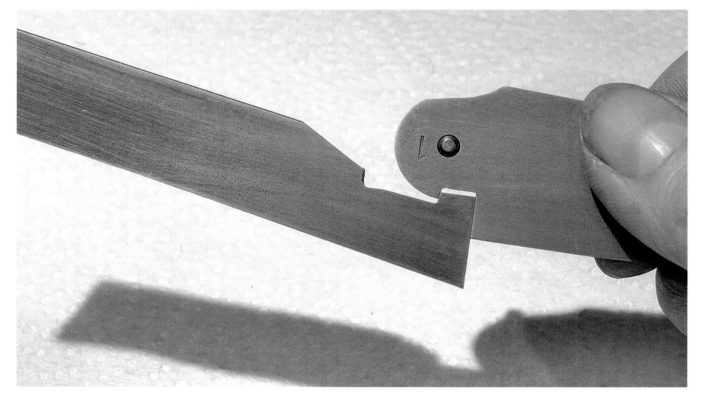

Finish the milled surface with abrasive paper. Again, use the blade to inspect the latch, testing the fit by joining the two parts. The two parts should hold together without assistance.

Options for the Blade Lock

There are various possibilities for the blade lock when the knife is closed. With a lockback the locking mechanism usually serves as the stop, which means that the inner outline of the locking mechanism and the ramp of the blade work together.

Alternatively, you can use a separate stop pin. Both options have advantages and disadvantages. With the first, when the knife is closed, the curve on the base of the blade lies on an edge on the inner surface of the locking mechanism. Because the stop is not fixed—the locking mechanism moves on its pivot—the blade slides along the locking mechanism under pressure, which can lead to the cutting edge striking. That is the classic construction of a lockback knife.

In place of a curve, you can work an edge into the blade ramp so that the blade cannot move the locking mechanism beyond the stop and the cutting edge is kept away from the spine of the blade. This, however, is expensive to do and requires considerable planning.

The problem can be avoided by using an additional stop pin where the blade hits. The cutting edge cannot touch the back of the knife. We have decided on the classic version in which the blade ramp hits the locking mechanism at a certain point. For lockback knives that is a typical performance.

Adjust the latch and notch and finish (up to 600 grit). Then, determine the point for the locking mechanism pivot. The pivot is located in the center of the locking mechanism. Place the locking mechanism into the liners, secure the blade, and trace the outline of the liners. Close to the midpoint of the liner draw a guideline. The position varies according to the amount of space you would like for locking and whether the locking mechanism will be short (functioning at the middle of the handle) or long (functioning at the end of the handle). In our case the amount of space for locking on the blade amounts to approximately 2 mm; a 1:1 gear ratio is sufficient.

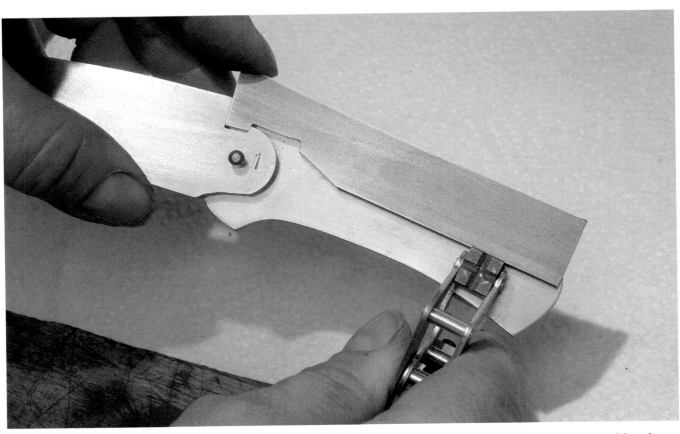

Position the blade in the open position and the latch engages the notch. Here we fixed the locking mechanism with a clamp.

Mark the outside of the locking mechanism along the liner.

Place the pivot on this centered guideline and at least 1 mm from the top edge of the liner. For the pivot we will use a 2.0 mm dowel pin. The pivot position is marked and pre-drilled with a 1.8 mm bit. Then, fix the locking mechanism into the desired position on the liners, which are still joined together and finish drilling the pivot hole. Ream the hole to 2.0 mm. Insert the dowel and check the functionality.

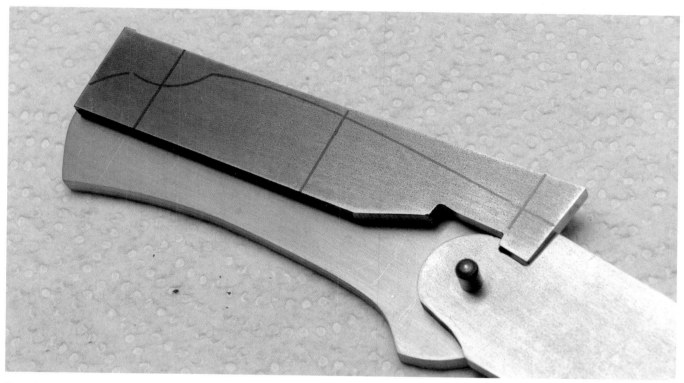

Roughly mark the center of the locking mechanism.

Pre-drill the pivot hole with a 1.8 mm bit.

Position and clamp the locking mechanism to a drilling jig and drill through the liners.

Then ream the drill holes to 2.0 mm.

In the next step you will shape the outer outline of the locking mechanism. Use the belt grinder to work along the traced outline of the handle liners. You can also file the outline. In a completely assembled state, finish the parts and make certain the outer outlines of the liners and locking mechanism are consistent. You can plan on touching these junctions up after the locking mechanism is hardened. That process may distort the dimensions of your components and/or deposit a layer of scale.

Use the belt grinder on the outer outline.

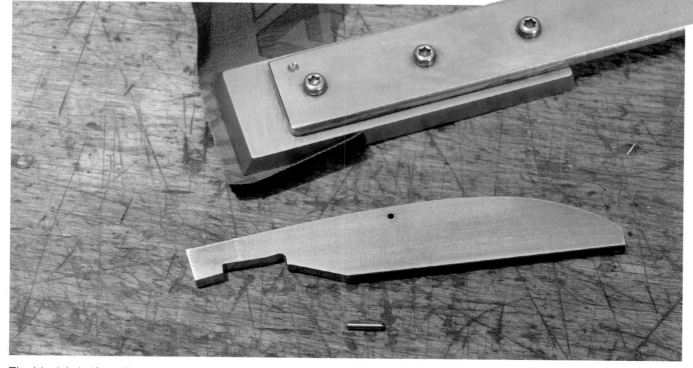

The blank is halfway finished. Before working on the inner outline, make sure all surfaces are ground and finished.

Swivel the blade into position and trace the cutting edge on the locking mechanism. Now we have a general idea of where we should place our stop and how much space remains for the spacer and spring.

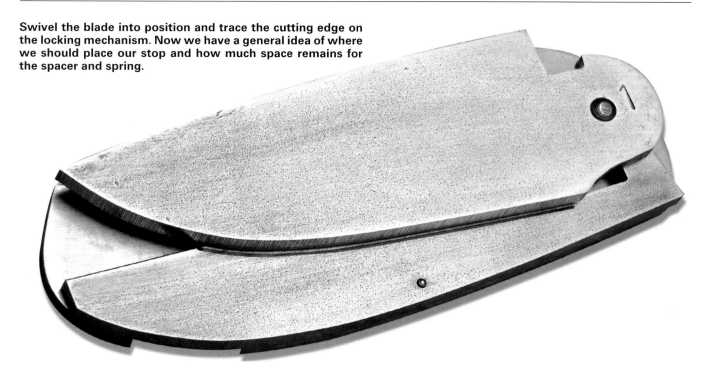

To work out the inner surface of the locking mechanism, assemble the blade and liners. Pay attention to the blade outline when the knife is closed. This will indicate the shape and length of the blade. You can now see how much space you will need for the locking mechanism, spring, and spacer. Mark the outline of the cutting edge with the blade closed.

Establish an edge where you will later insert the spring. The spring should function approximately 5-10 mm behind the pivot, either as an integrated component, in which the locking mechanism and spring form one unit, or as separate piece to insert.

At this point you should chose whether the spring is fixed in the spacer and is operated on the locking mechanism, or, like in the version we present here, the spring is fixed in the locking mechanism and functions on the spacer. The advantage of this solution is that it requires less operating force. For a secure locking mechanism the power of a slightly pre-stressed spring is completely sufficient.

Choose a spring that is as long as possible to minimize stress on the piece. We should note that your spring material should be slightly pre-stressed. Take the space requirements into account and choose the shape of the spacer accordingly.

Sketch the spacer, which will incorporate the spring in a later step. Now, mark the recesses on the liners that operate the spring. The thickness of the locking mechanism should mask these.

Later we will develop the blade lock. Therefore, as a precaution, we will leave some excess material behind the latch.

The inner outline of the locking mechanism is now complete. Drill along the outlines, separate the remaining material with a saw, and mill the surface flat. Because the end of the locking mechanism moves around the pivot in a circular path, mark the radius accurately with a compass. This prevents gaps that will affect the knife's operation.

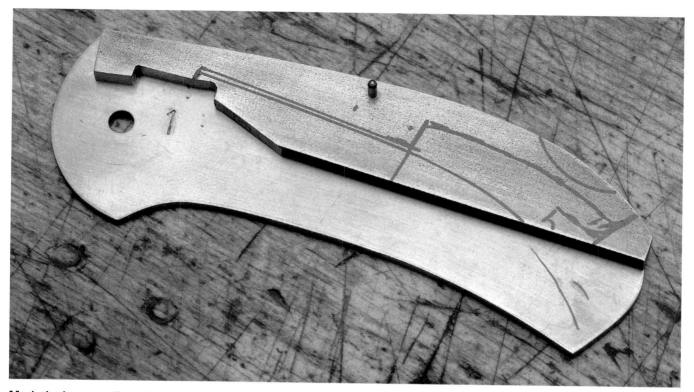

Mark the inner outline. Make the back section of the locking mechanism so that sufficient space remains for a spring. In the front area leave enough material to make later adjustments on the blade lock.

Drill a row of holes along the outline to remove the material.

Milling the inner outline. A file or belt grinder can also be used.

Touch up the outlines with a belt grinder and fine-tune the edges with a file and abrasive paper.

Now assemble the spring. Guidelines help clamp in the locking mechanism so you can drill as vertically as possible. Depending on the shape of the locking mechanism, the length of the drill bit, and the size of the chuck, you may not be able to drill at a right angle. But this is irrelevant because the spring can be appropriately bent afterwards.

For the spring we will use 2.0 mm round stock. Therefore we will drill our holes with a 1.8 mm bit and then ream to 2.0 mm. First, temporarily insert the spring.

Mark the end of the locking mechanism with a compass.

Roughly prepare the inner outline with a belt grinder.

Touch up the locking mechanism with a file, then precision grind by hand with abrasive paper (up to 400 grit).

Sketch the location of the drill hole for the spring. It may not be possible to drill a perfectly perpendicular hole from above. To determine this before you start drilling, place a rail along the marked drill hole.

To test operation and fit, fix the slightly pre-stressed spring with a small bar clamp. If necessary, you may need to touch up the locking mechanism piece. This is especially true for the lock. Does the latch catch while closing, does it run neatly on the blade ramp? For ideal functionality precision grind the surface with 600 grit or higher.

With an extended 1.8 mm drill bit (the drill chuck must be able to go past the end of the locking mechanism) drill the hole for the spring.

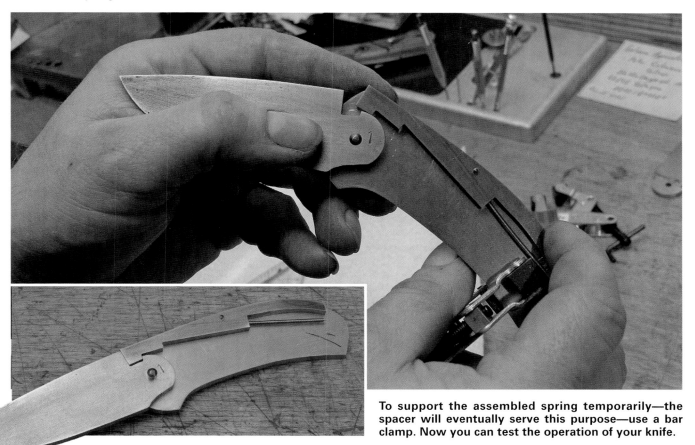

To support the assembled spring temporarily—the spacer will eventually serve this purpose—use a bar clamp. Now you can test the operation of your knife.

6. The Blade Lock

Work carefully and use small steps when making adjustments on the various components of your knife. Regularly checking how the knife works is important. With the next steps you must decide how and where the blade will be drawn into the knife and retained when closing.

As previously mentioned, there are two versions:

1. **Stopped on the locking mechanism:** In this version the blade is in direct contact with the bottom edge of the locking mechanism. Remember that we left excess material on the locking mechanism to make accurate adjustment to the blade. Examine the proportions with your functional template. You must pay attention to several parameters simultaneously with these steps. For example, while adjusting the blade ramp with the edges in the locking mechanism, you must also apply pressure on the blade, triggering the latch to pull it into the handle. Additionally, the upper edge of the locking mechanism, when open and closed, should be flush with the handle.

2. **Additional stop pin:** First, consider where sufficient space remains for a stop pin. You can place it behind the blade pivot without any problems. Mark the desired location beforehand and make sure adjusting the base of the blade does not have a disruptive affect in this spot when open. To accommodate a suitable dowel pin with a 3.0 mm diameter, pre-drill with a 2.8 mm bit and then ream the holes to 3.0 mm. Grind the base of the blade until the stop fits. Now, adjust the outline of the locking mechanism in both open and closed positions onto the liners. Tip: This version can still save a knife when the stop above the locking mechanism is not successful.

Advice: If too much material is removed from the base of the blade, the locking mechanism will reach too far into the liners. To make corrections you must adjust the liners accordingly.

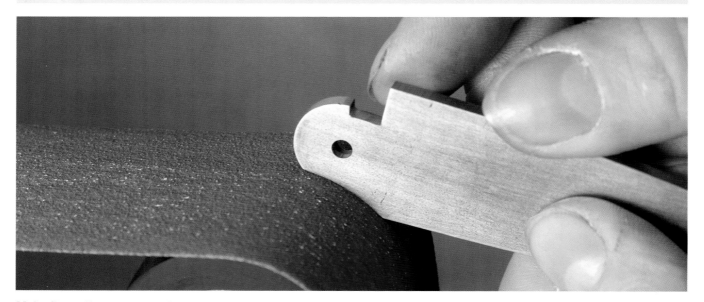

Make fine adjustments to the parts by removing material with a belt grinder. But make sure you leave enough material for subsequent adjustments.

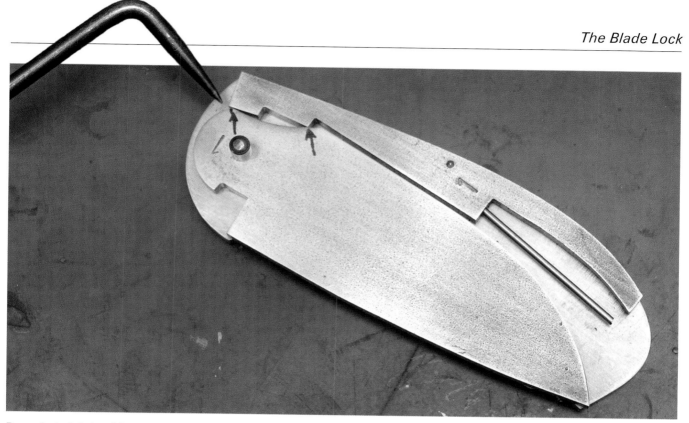

Draw in helpful guide points. The arrow on the left marks the location where the force of the spring pushes the latch into a stopped position when the knife is closed—this pushes the blade into the handle. The rear edge behind the latch serves as a stop for the blade.

Draw in helpful guide points on the blade. The front point marks the area where the latch should press to pull in the blade. This edge may not be removed. The back point marks the position where the blade hits. Here we remove material until the blade is in the handle and the locking mechanism is simultaneously flush with the back of the handle. The radius in between is necessary so the blade can move freely.

Add the markings and grind the ramp on a contact wheel. Proceed carefully and test the operation after each work step.

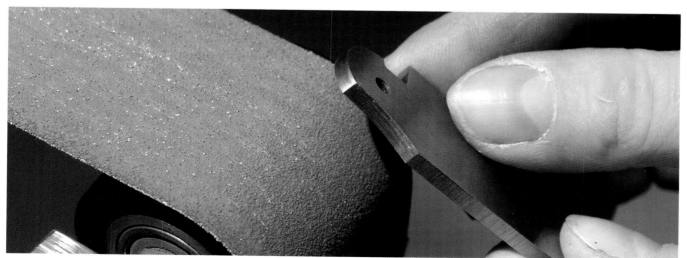

Step by step work towards the appropriate outline. Keep in mind that your parts still need to be precision ground (up to 600 grit). Therefore, continue to leave some excess material. One point to note: with 0.1 to 0.2 mm of excess material the latch is still not flush with the handle.

7. Making the Spacer

Important Information Regarding the Spacer

The spacer in a lockback mechanism can have many functions. Depending on the knife's design a spacer can have two basic styles. If the spacer joins the handle scales and additionally serves as a support or secure mounting for the spring, this must be taken into consideration during design. If the spring rests on an additional stop pin incorporated into the knife, you are less restricted with the design of the spacer. This produces a knife with a more open back. You can secure the spacer in various ways, regardless of whether you use a roll pin.

1. First, drill a clearance hole through the spacer. In one side of the liners drill a clearance hole (with a counterbore), in the other a thread. You will fix the liners and the spacers together with this screw and possibly several other screws. In addition, pin the spacer for exact positioning.

2. Drill a thread into the clearance holes in the spacer and liners. From both sides the spacer is screwed together with the liners. You should pin it as well.

In our knife the spacer assumes two functions: it combines the liners and at the same time serves as a support and working point for the spring. We use the RWL-34 material that will later be hardened. The thickness is equal to that of the blade plus both washers. Use the most appropriate flat stock so you do not have to spend a lot of time flat grinding.

On the inner surface of the liner, mark the area where the spacer should be located. Mark the spring support on the spacer and work out this edge (saw, file, mill, etc.). Now, temporarily fix the spacer onto the liners with the help of a bar clamp. In the correct position the spring should bend forward slightly (if it does not you should bend the spring accordingly) and the spacer should be flush to the end of the locking mechanism. Briefly test the operation.

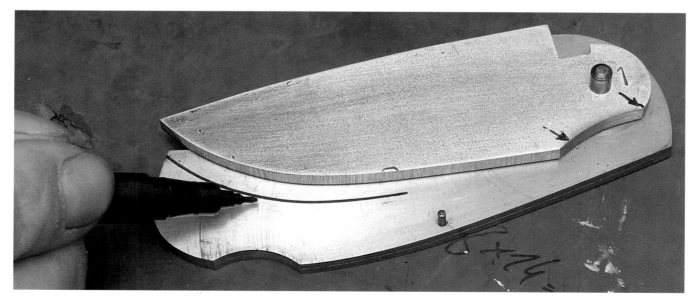

Mark the area where the spacer, spring, and locking mechanism are located. Then mark the area that remains when the blade is closed.

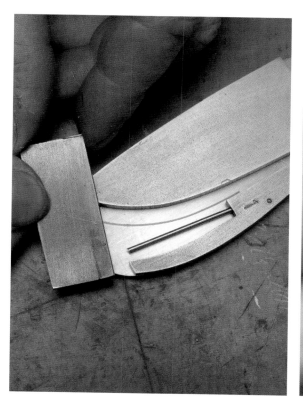 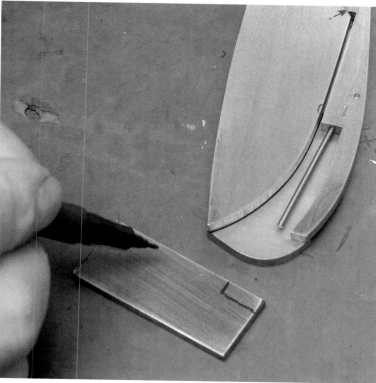

Assemble the locking mechanism and spring. Determine the dimensions of the recess where the spring will be positioned, and mark it.

Mill out a small notch in the spacer (you can also use a file).

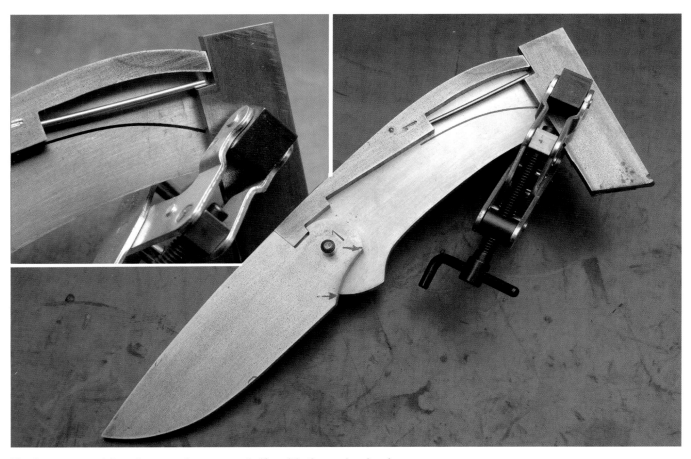

Fix the spacer with a clamp and test your knife with the spring in place.

With the spacer still clamped, drill and ream the hole for the first dowel pin through the spacer and both liners (1.5 mm dowel pin). Transfer the outline of the handle end onto the spacer and fix the spacer with another dowel pin. In addition, drill a clearance hole for the liner screws. For this one place a counterbore, the other receives a thread. To drill the thread accurately, we use an auxiliary device to keep the hole vertical. You can use this auxiliary equipment later when drilling for the handle scales.

Above: **Drill the spacer with the liner using a 1.3 mm bit.**

Left: **Ream the hole to 1.5 mm for the dowel pin. Do not forget to use cutting oil.**

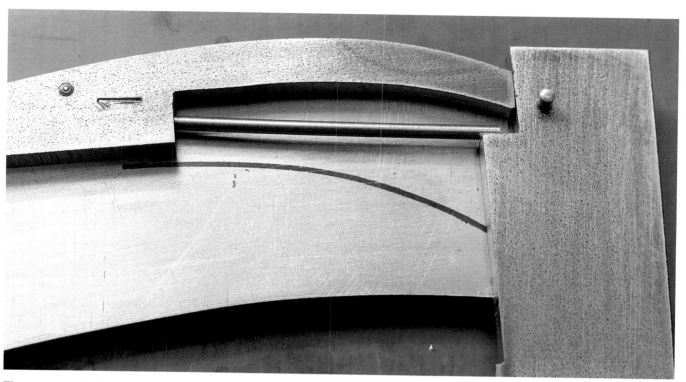

The spacer with the dowel pin in place. The spring is bent slightly upward.

Place the second dowel pin and drill a clearance hole for an M2 screw.

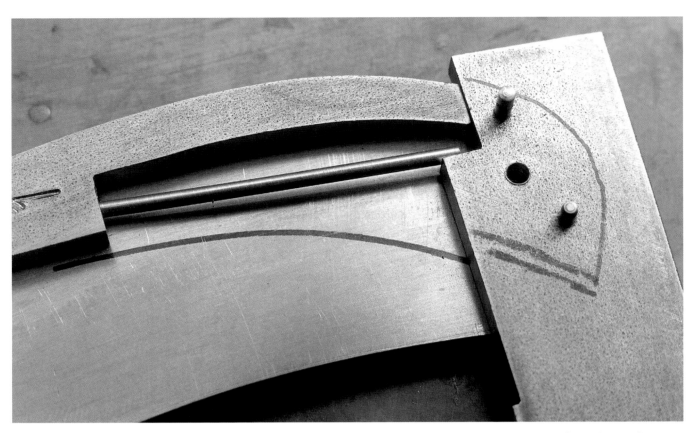

Mount the spacer and trace the outlines of the handle and the blade. Remove some more material from the cutting area so the cutting edge does not bump against the spacer later.

Roughly cut the outline with a hacksaw.

Finish the shape of the spacer, using a hacksaw for the preliminary work. With the dowel pins placed in the liners, use the belt grinder to work out the outline of the handle.

As mentioned before, inspect the dimensions for your spacer and locking mechanism—the width should be equal to the blade thickness plus two washers. The thickness of the spacer must be exact, otherwise the frame will not be straight and the knife will not function properly. Use an abrasive paper on an even base, like a pane of glass, to finish the flat surfaces of these parts.

Your final adjustments to the locking mechanism will take place after the heat treatment process to address possible distortion.

The locking mechanism should move easily between the liners.

Left: Use a belt grinder to finish the spacer's outline.

Below: The drilled spacer. You will precision finish the work by hand later when it is mounted.

Grind the spacer and locking mechanism to the same thickness on a cup grinding machine. Use leftover materials to hold your knife in place.

8. Grinding the Blade

Fix the blade to the knife frame with a dowel pin. Then open the knife and mark the end of the grind and the spot where the grinding should proceed to the ricasso. You can grind the marks out later.

Now mark the center of the blade on the underside of the blade. This will later become the cutting edge.

Tip: Tracing against the grind line is more visible. Grind lightly over the underside of the blade.

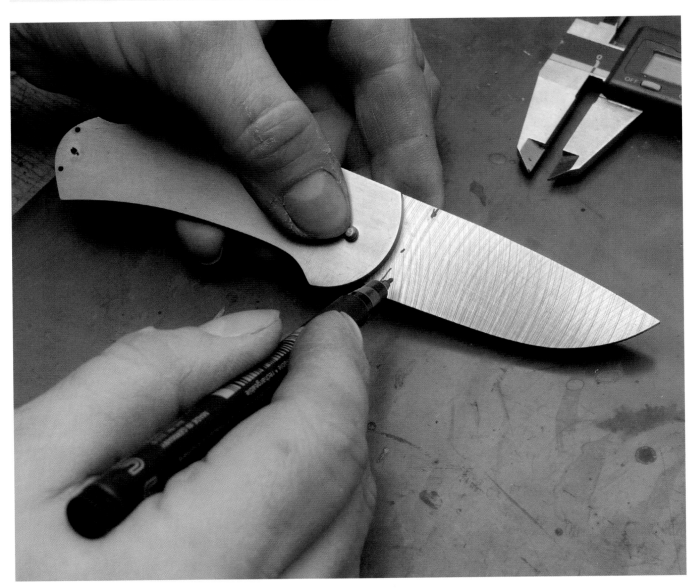

Mark the end of the grind on the blade with a marker.

To make sure the markings are parallel on both sides, clamp the blade into a vise and trace along the vice pads on both sides.

Using a height gauge, mark the center of the blade, which will become the cutting edge.

The marked blade. The next step of the process takes place at the belt grinder, but you can also use a file.

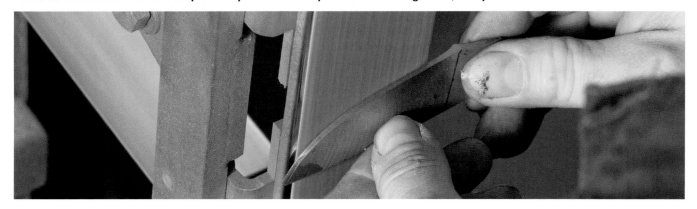

Grinding the blade

Use the belt grinder to surface grind the blade, extending the grind continuously to the spine of the blade. This produces a flat grinding angle and enhances your knife's cutting properties.

Start with a coarse abrasive belt (60-80 grit). For the precision grinding use a flexible belt (150-240 grit) that you can place into the ricasso. Make sure that the edges do not wear away. You can also use a file and an abrasive block.

Leave between 0.2 mm and 0.5 mm of material on the cutting edge. You will finish grinding the blade after the blade is hardened.

Your roughly ground blade should clearly show that you have adhered to the marked boundaries.

Complete the precision grinding and finishing by hand, starting with 240 grit and working your way to 400 and then 600. Do not forget to grind the spine of the blade.

Work carefully at the junction from the spine to the notch. The edges must remain sharp and should not be worn down. You may find it helpful to finish the grinding after your knife is assembled.

In addition to the blade, grind the locking mechanism with 600 grit. Once all of your components are hand-finished take them to be hardened at a heat treatment shop.

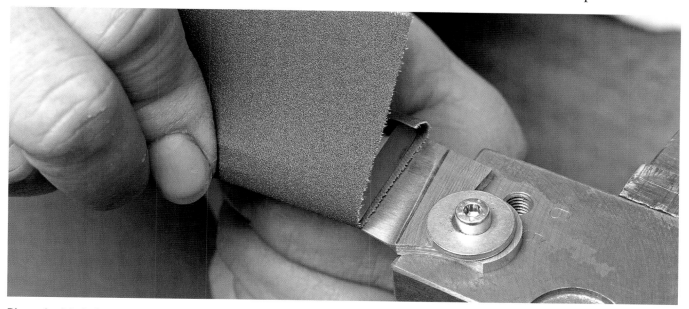

Place the blade in a vise and continue the finishing work by hand with an abrasive block.

When grinding, pay careful attention to the edges so you do not wear them down.

Blade, locking mechanism, and spacer, ready for the heat treatment shop.

Four Tips for Finishing

- A high quality abrasive paper will last longer and allow you to achieve a better finish.

- Before switching to the next finest grit, the finish must be flawless and even.

- Each time you switch to a finer grit, change the direction you are grinding in. Grinding is done best grit by grit at a 90° angle to the previous grade.

- Pay attention to creating neat, clean edges (especially the junction to the ricasso along the spine of the blade). Do not grind round.

9. Making the Bolsters

As mentioned earlier, there are various options for making the bolsters. We will concentrate on the versions in which the blade pivot extends through the bolsters and is thus accessible externally. The bolsters are mounted with two secure dowel pins. The blade pivot maintains the construction.

Alternatively, you can conceal the blade pivot. For this a notch is included on the inner surface of the bolsters that incorporates the blade pivot. The bolsters are then screwed together with the liners. You can also use continuous handle scales with either a hidden or visible blade pivot.

Cut the raw material to the appropriate length. Later your bolsters should have a tapered radius to join cleanly with the handle scales. Mark the center on the liner and trace the radius onto the liners with a compass.

With the aid of the liners sketch the outlines of the bolsters and mark the drill hole for the pivot. Leave sufficient material for the radius.

For a 4.0 mm pivot, drill first with a 3.8 mm bit and ream the drill hole to 4.0 mm. Fix the bolsters together with instant adhesive or a bar clamp so that the drill hole is perpendicular and both bolsters are drilled out simultaneously.

With a 12.0 mm counterbore, drill a hole on both sides where the blade screw should hit the bottom. Leave 2.0 mm on the bottom to be able to insert a dowel pin, which will later serve as a locking device for the pivot.

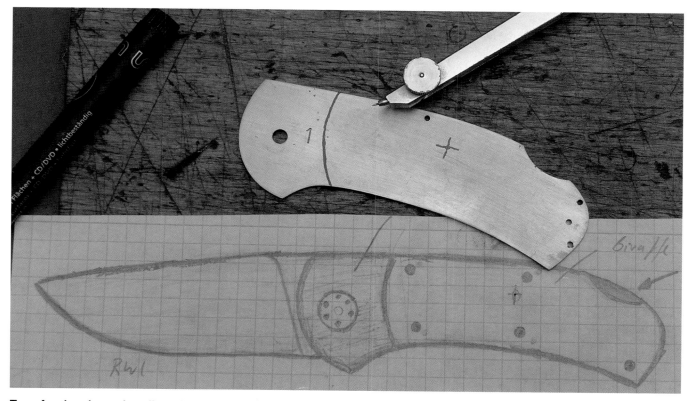

Transfer the planned outline of the bolsters from the sketch onto the liners.

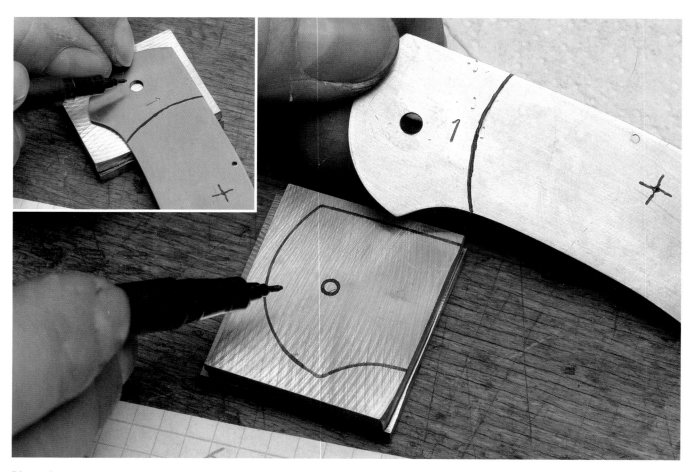

Place the liners on the bolster material, mark the outline, and then drill the hole for the pivot.

Drill the pivot hole. Fix the bolsters to each other with instant adhesive and drill through both pieces at the same time.

With a dowel pin, fix both bolsters on a liner and trace the outline. To make a rough cut out of the shape, use a cut-off wheel then continue working out the shape on the belt grinder.

Drill a center hole through both liners on the marked location so that you can clamp the liners together with the bolsters on the rotary table later.

Because you will attach the bolsters securely with two pins (1.5 mm), pre-drill into the liners with a 1.3 mm bit. Make sure the drill holes are outside the notch of the blade pivot.

Separate the liners and bolsters for the right and left sides and mount the bolsters onto the liners, straighten them, and continue drilling through the existing drill holes. Then ream to 1.5 mm and pin the bolsters to the liners.

Clamp the liners with the pinned bolsters to the rotary table—a dowel pin through the center hole serves as a centering tool. Now, mill the radius with a 90° end mill and then the angles in the notch with a 15° dovetail mill.

Remove the bolsters from the liners and neatly grind them. Adjust the height of the bolsters on the liners using a file and abrasive paper.

Ream the drill hole to the required dimension of 4.0 mm.

Set your counterbore with a depth stop and mill into the notch for the pivot on both sides. Your counterbore should be deep enough to include the entire pivot head according to the radius of the bolsters. We are using a depth of 2 mm.

Transfer the outline of the handle onto the bolsters with a scriber.

Make the preliminary cuts with either an angle grinder or a hacksaw.

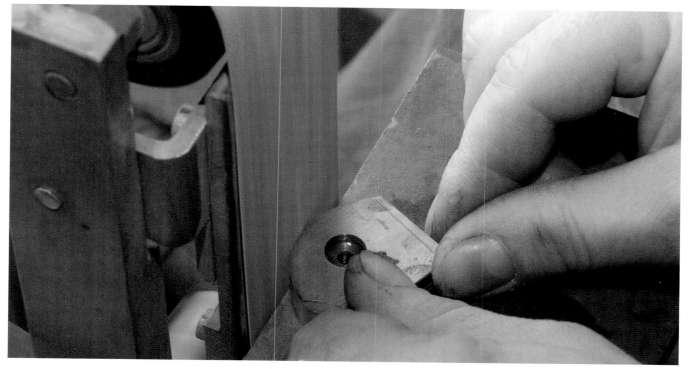

Work out the outline of the bolsters with a belt grinder.

After the belt grinder your bolsters with the notch should look like this.

Dowel pins are required to fix the bolsters to the liners in a later step. Here holes are pre-drilled into the liners.

Fix the bolsters in the proper position on the liners with a dowel pin and instant adhesive. Pre-drill through the liners. Do not drill to deep because the bolsters will be rounded off later.

Ream the drill hole through the liners and bolsters in one step.

Match up the liners and bolsters accurately and pin them together.

Now drill and ream a hole to center the piece on the rotary table.

Securely clamp the piece and start milling the radius with a 90° end mill.

Use a 15° dovetail mill on the side for the handle junction.

The undefined bolsters. Remove the burrs after milling.

To curve the bolsters, clamp them into auxiliary equipment on the belt grinder. Use 80/150 grit on the grinder followed by an abrasive block and paper. Neatly round the edges for a more refined look

Finish the bolsters by hand, rounding the edges and grinding the outline with abrasive paper (200/400/600). On the side where the blade pivot will later be located, drill and ream a hole for the dowel pin, which will serve as a locking device for the pivot. After this send the bolsters to a heat treatment shop.

Round the bolsters on the grinding equipment.

A view of the grinding from above.

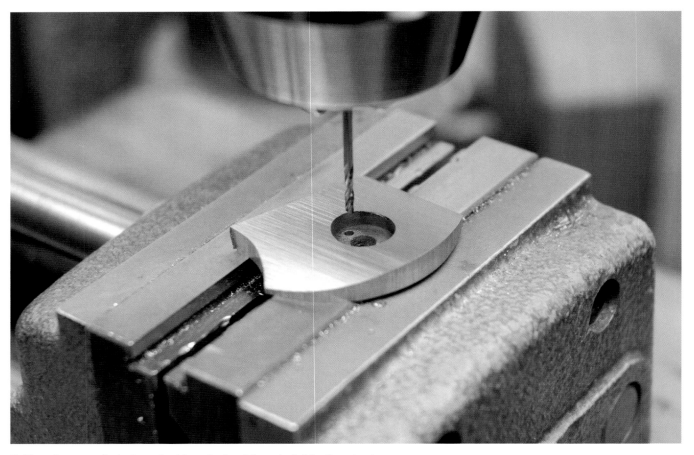

Drill and ream a hole for a locking device (dowel pin) in the pivot.

Adjust the bolsters on the liners, round the edges, and finish with precision grinding.

10. The Blade Pivot

We will make the pivot out of a solid piece of titanium and finish it on the lathe. If this equipment is not available, you can use either prefabricated parts or improvise. For example, you can make pivots from various ornamental screws.

Material: If you use steel for the pivot, its hardness should be approximately five to ten Rockwell levels below the blade. Using unhardened steel should be sufficient—hardening increases the risk of distortion and does not offer any advantages when used in low stress conditions. Alternatively, brass, titanium, and bronze are also suitable. If desired, you can also use a steel pivot and set a bronze bushing into the blade. The advantage here is that this creates a self-lubricating blade mounting, however, this requires great precision and more steps.

To get started on the pivot, first, determine its length. This dimension should be the thickness of the blade, washers, the liners, and the bolsters. You must also consider the depth of the notches in the bolsters. In our knife they are 11.5 mm.

Now there are two possibilities:

1. **We work on the fit.** The length of the pivot corresponds to the above base measurement. The end of the pivot is exactly flush with the bottom of the counterbore in the bolsters. This requires extremely accurate work. The blade action of a completed knife cannot be adjusted without a great deal of modification. The charm of this version is having everything fit exactly.

2. **The pivot ends approximately .05 mm below the bottom of the counterbore.** This gives us some play during production. The blade play can be adjusted later by raising the pivot with the screw.

In contrast to the first option, with the second version a locking device is absolutely necessary, either with positive locking or by adhering the pivot with a thread locker. In this project we decide to use a dowel pin as a positive locking device. For this version the length for the pivot is 11.0 mm.

First, clamp the titanium blank into the lathe. Then drill an M3 internal thread. The material can bulge from tapping, but you can take care of this later when you turn the piece on the lathe. For this we drill a center hole then the core hole and the thread. Turn the shaft of the pivot to a diameter of 4.0 mm first, and then turn the head of the pivot to 12.0 mm. Work in small steps and test the measurement frequently, placing the blade onto the shaft of the pivot after each step.

Using a lathe, place a center hole in the titanium pivot.

Drill the thread after drilling the core hole.

Then turn the pivot to the desired diameters.

Carefully turn the piece, regularly testing its diameter with the blade.

Finally, separate the pivot from the rest of the material.

Now clamp what remains of the titanium blank and strip the front end.

To make the screw end of the pivot, turn the blank to 3.0 mm in diameter and then cut the thread.

Complete the screw end of the pivot (screw head 12.0 mm, thread diameter M3). Then clamp both turned parts, and turn them flat to the correct length. For this knife both ends of the pivot are slightly counterbored in the bolsters.

Now drill five holes in the head of the screw end of the pivot. Make sure you do not drill the counterbores too deeply so the holes do not push through the bottom of the pivot head.

To complete the locking device, place the pivot into the bolsters. The previously drilled holes make a recess on the inner surface of the pivot. Mark the position of the locking pin so you can adjust the pivot accordingly.

Use an auxiliary tool with an M3 internal thread to finish working on the screw.

To drill the front holes, clamp the pivot and screw into a dividing head.

Drill the front holes one by one.

Slightly counterbore the holes in the pivot. Grind the top surface to remove the burrs.

Mark the position of the locking device so you can adjust the pivot accordingly. This ensures that the hole on the opposite side does not collide with the front holes.

Drill a hole in the bolsters for the locking device according to the alignment of the pivot.

Both ends of the pivot and the locking pin.

11. Customizing the Handle

Mount the bolsters onto the liners and mark the junction of the handle scales using the liners as a template. Make sure the handle scale material is large enough for our liners and then cut the outline around the handle scales.

Similar to the production of the bolsters, add a radius to the handle scales. Mark the center hole through the liner, which will assist us when making adjustments on the milling machine.

After drilling, grind the inside of the handle scales flat by placing abrasive paper on a flat surface like a pane of glass.

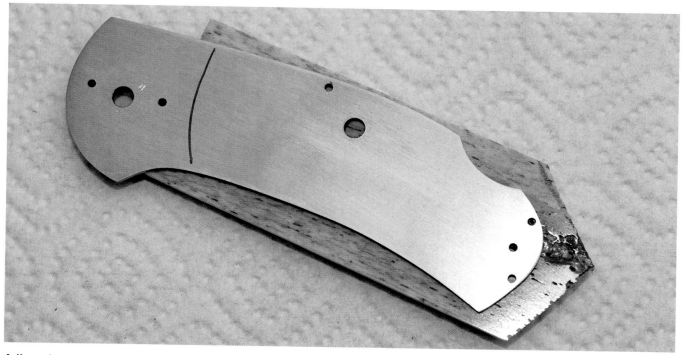

Adjust the handle material on the liners so that enough excess material remains all around for fine-tuning.

Mark the center hole on the handle material.

Drill a blind hole, but only deep enough for a dowel pin. If the drill hole is too deep, you run the risk of grinding through the drill hole when you later round out the handle material.

Grind the handle material flat.

Using the center hole you marked earlier, clamp the handle material on the rotary table. Set the bit to the dovetail angle you used earlier and mill the same radius as the bolsters.

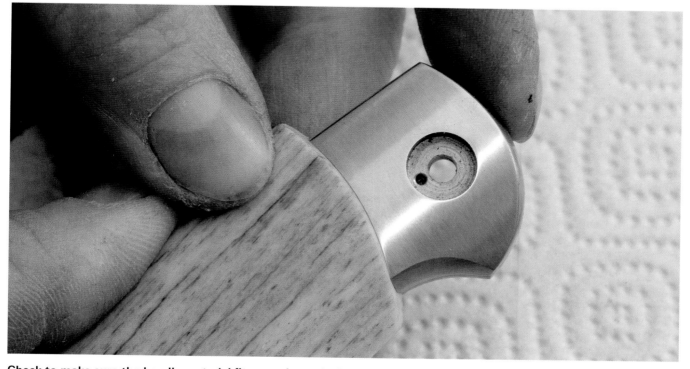

Check to make sure the handle material fits exactly on the bolsters and touch up by hand if necessary.

Clamp the handle material on the rotary table. Like the bolsters, set the milling head to a 15° angel and gradually work on the desired radius. Regularly check the fit with the bolsters.

Mount the bolsters on the liners and correctly adjust the dowel pin. Mark the positions for the drill holes, which will later screw together with the handle scales, and drill the core hole for the thread. For the M3 thread drill with a 2.5 mm bit. Enlarge the drill holes on the outside of the liners.

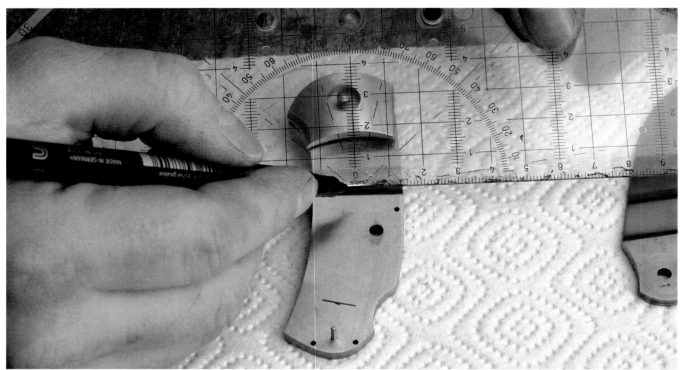

Mark the positions for the drill holes, which will later screw together with the handle scales.

Drill tapping holes for the M3 thread (2.5 mm).

Left: For the subsequent mounting you will need a clearance hole with a counterbore on one side of the liners. Later there will be a screw through this hole that joins both liners with each other. Drill the same clearance hole that we used producing the spacer (1.6 mm to 2.0 mm). *Right:* Then counterbore the through-hole.

Drill the M2 thread into the liner on the opposite side with alignment support.

Place the handle scales on the liners. They will be fixed over collets and must fit exactly on the bolsters. Then, use the liners as a drilling jig and drill 2.5 mm clearance holes through the handle scales.

Drill the handle material with 3.0 mm for the screws and enlarge the holes. Because we size the heads of the M3 screws for our knife to 5.0 mm, we use a 5.0 mm counterbore.

Cut the M3 thread into the liners using a centering tool and cutting oil.

Size the screw heads and adjust their length accordingly. To bring the screws to their correct length we have made an auxiliary device that we can use to shorten the screws with a file.

Clamp the liners and scales together.

Using the tapping drill hole as a template, drill the holes for the screws into the handle material.

Finally, drill the holes to 3.0 mm.

Enlarge the drill holes for the screw heads with the counterbore.

Drill the M3 thread into the liner with alignment support.

Size the screw heads to 5.0 mm so they are consistent with the counterbore.

Using abrasive paper, remove any traces of work on the liners and handle scales before mounting the handle scales. With the belt grinder, finish the outline of the liners. As before you can also use a file and abrasive paper. Finally, finish the piece by precision grinding by hand with abrasive paper.

Work on the junction of the handle scales to the bolsters separately. Wood and other natural materials are ground much more quickly than the hardened steel of the bolsters. If you work both at the same time, the junctions will not be neat and even.

Mount the handle scales on the liners with the bolsters.

Work the outline of the handle scales on the belt grinder. You can also use the grinder to start rounding the surfaces of the scales. As you work the handle scales, make sure the scales are the same thickness.

After the belt grinder, complete the work by hand for a more precise finish.

Now use a file and abrasive paper to make more exact adjustments to the handle material. Caution: using a belt grinder, it is easy to remove too much material too quickly.

You can use shaped tools to finish the recess in the handle.

Preliminary results. Only the washers and the final finish are missing.

12. Making the Washers

To complete the assembly of your knife you need the appropriate washers. Teflon or bronze is typically used for this part. The washers should have the largest possible diameter, as much as the design of the knife allows, so the contact pressure is spread out as widely as possible. This allows the blade to run more smoothly, and the blade action can be better adjusted.

Teflon: You can easily produce Teflon washers. With punch pliers and scissors you can cut or punch the raw material into the desired diameter. You can use either pure or fiber-reinforced Teflon in a variety of thicknesses.

Teflon washers can pick up small particles of dirt. However, with small diameters Teflon cannot absorb much pressure and the lateral stability is not very good. Thus, you may have to reinforce the blade, which in turn makes the blade action stiff.

Bronze: Washers made of bronze are costly to make. You can punch holes in bronze sheet metal, roughly cut out the pieces, clamp them onto a pin, and turn them. To punch holes in the bronze sheet metal we use a specially made punch tool. Finished bronze washers are only available in a few sizes.

Bronze washers are more susceptible to dirtying and are not as resilient as Teflon. Also, with bronze washers small particles of dirt easily get into the blade. The advantage of a bronze washer is that it is more dimensionally stable than washers made of Teflon. Thus, you can adjust the blade action more finely. The adjustment is also maintained over a long period of time and the blade action is more precise. Additionally, bronze washers have a self-lubricating effect.

A homemade punch tool used to produce bronze washers at various punch diameters according to the pivot.

Roughly cut the washers to shape.

Clamp the square pieces onto a pin for turning.

Then, turn the washers on a lathe.

Use this process to make washers in every desired diameter.

To make bronze washers, sheet metal in various thicknesses and composition are available, including bearing bronze and tin bronze. The material thickness of the washers depends on how exact the fit should be with a knife. Thicknesses of 0.1 mm or 0.2 mm are commonly used for knives. If more space is desired, use thicknesses from 0.3 mm to 0.5 mm.

You could also do without washers. In that situation the blade runs directly on the liners. To use this method you need an optimal surface finish. Additionally, the sliding surface, here the liners, should be at least 5-10 HRC less than the blade. Liners made of Titanium, steel, or nonferrous metal are suitable for this. There are disadvantages to this design. The surface treatment for these metals is costly, it is susceptible to the smallest particles of dirt, and the materials can be uneven.

13. Design Variations

We made six different versions of our lockback folding knife. They are different in material, length, and locking mechanism design. The knives also differ in the presence of bolsters, as well as the visibility of the blade pivot. The different technical aspects of the versions are illustrated here. The knife that is most visually appealing to you is a matter of taste.

1. Mosaic Damascus / Mother of Pearl

This knife features a long locking mechanism and a spring made out of round stock that is fixed in the locking mechanism and supported by an extra stop pin. The pivot is hidden under the bolsters. On the inner side of the bolsters we included a corresponding notch.

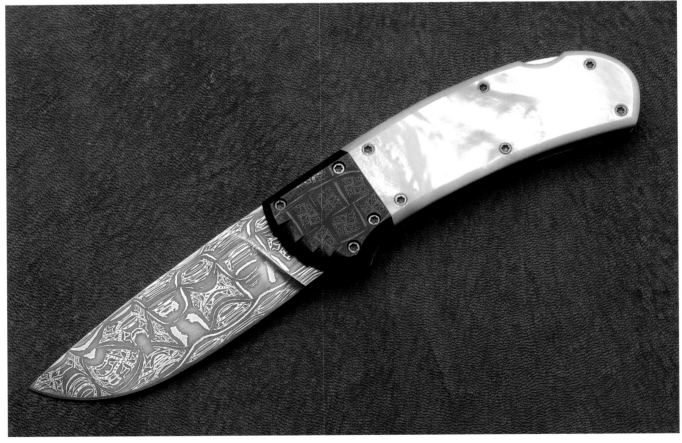

2. RWL-34 / Giraffe Bone (stabilized) / Clip

On this knife we included a long locking mechanism and a handle with bolsters, pinned and held with the pivot screw. The knife has two interesting details: first, an extra stop pin (3.0 mm dowel pin) for the blade lock. Second, the spring (flat stock 3x1.5) is fixed in the locking mechanism and does not rest on the spacer but rather an extra pin (3.0 mm dowel). Thus, a small roll pin can be used as a spacer. We also made a clip for this knife.

We screwed the clip on from the inside through the bolsters. Therefore you cannot see the screws on the outside of the knife.

In other versions the clip is screwed on from the outside. A roll pin or solid material serves as a spacer.

3. RWL-34 / Giraffe Bone (stabilized)

Here we have a knife with a long locking mechanism and a spring made of round stock that is fixed in the locking mechanism and rests on the spacer. This is the knife that we described in detail throughout this book.

4. Olivine Meteorite / Interior frame

The liners are made from RWL-34 with an interior frame construction and integrated bolsters. To reduce the weight of this knife, we added notches. The knife has a long locking mechanism and the round stock spring is fixed in the locking mechanism and rests on the spacer.

5. RWL-34 / Mammoth-Ivory

This knife also has an interior frame design. To reduce the weight of the knife, we added a round notch. With this knife the locking mechanism and spring form one unit. The steel is 1.4034 and has a hardness of approximately 45 HRC. The spring rests on the spacer. To operate the spring, the locking mechanism is serrated on the end. An appropriate recess was included in the liner to accommodate this feature.

6. Damasteel Scale Knife / Ebony

This knife features a short locking mechanism. The flat stock spring stays in the spacer. The handle scales are identical since the pivot notches are hidden on the inside.

14. Finishing and Final Steps

Once you receive the blade and bolsters from the heat treatment shop, you can finish your knife. First, make sure that all parts function properly. If necessary, adjust the tension of the spring by bending it forward.

Next, jewel the inside of the liners. To produce an even pattern, we built a mounting device to complete the jewelling at even intervals. Fix the liners with glue or screw them on.

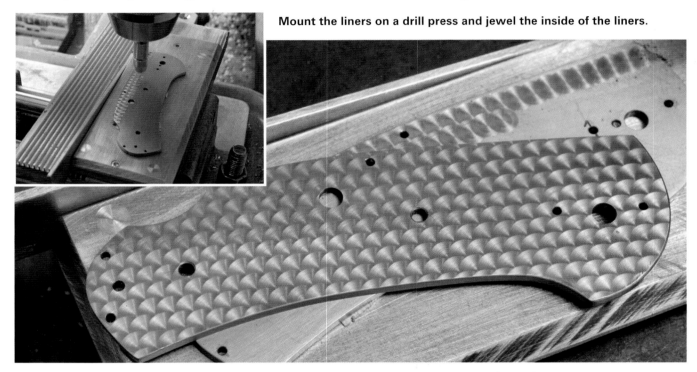

Mount the liners on a drill press and jewel the inside of the liners.

Give the blade a satin finish using abrasive paper. Grind evenly lengthwise with increasing grit numbers until you reach the desired finish. A steady hand and even movement is important here. You will notice a sideways or unsteady grind immediately.

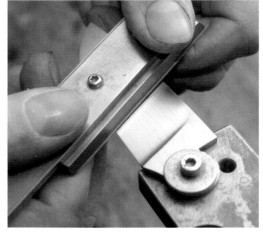

Put a satin finish on the blade, grinding lengthwise with fine abrasive paper (800 grit).

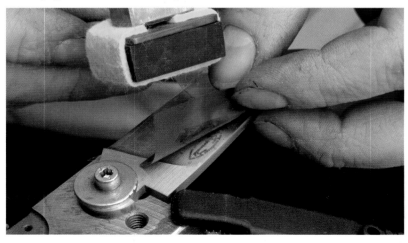

Stamping the blade with a logo using an electro-chemical etching.

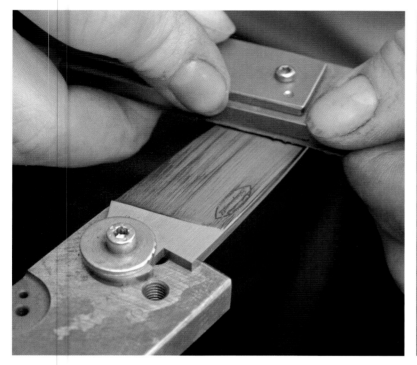

After etching, grind the blade once again with a diamond paste to bring out the etched logo.

Anodize the liners and small parts made of titanium. In an electrolyte apply voltage between anode and cathode. The 18-volt charge we used created a blue coloration.

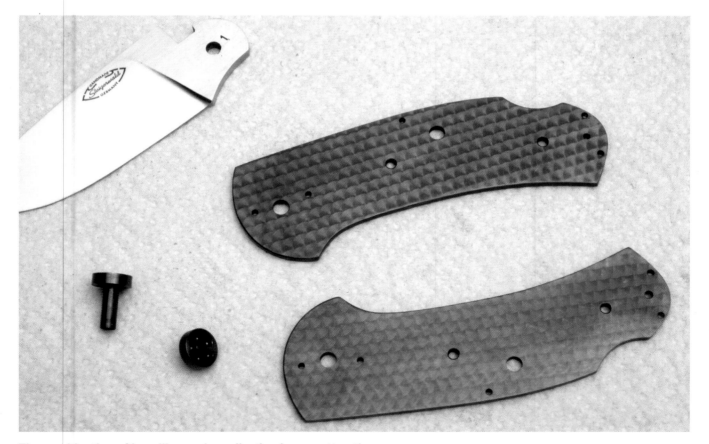

The combination of jewelling and anodization is very attractive.

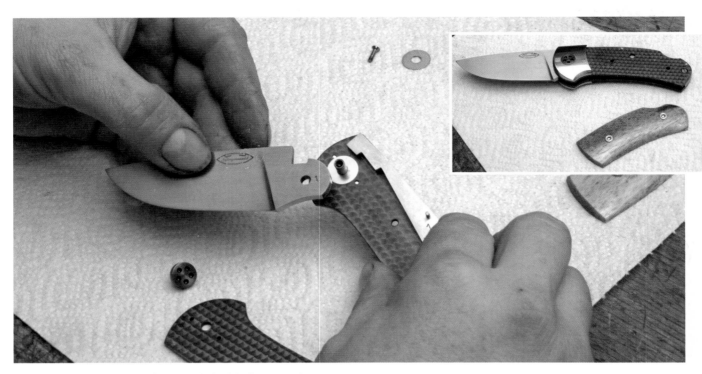

Finally, assemble the knife and oil the blade mounting.

Assemble the knife for inspection, checking the operation and fit. Correct any inaccuracies, at the junctions, for example.

Lightly lubricate the pivot and washers with non-resinous oil and assemble the knife. Secure all screws with medium strength threadlocker.

Your final step is to grind the blade with a diamond sharpener.

Now your knife is done!

Sharpen the blade with a diamond file.